Editors
Kim Fields
Heather Douglas

Managing Editor
Ina Massler Levin, M.A.

Illustrator
Vicki Frazier

Cover Artist
Tony Carillo

Art Production Manager
Kevin Barnes

Imaging
James Edward Grace

Publisher
Mary D. Smith, M.S. Ed.

Traits of Good Writing
Grades 1–2

Author
Tracie Heskett, M. Ed.

Teacher Created Resources, Inc.
6421 Industry Way
Westminster, CA 92683
www.teachercreated.com
ISBN-1-4206-3584-0
©2006 Teacher Created Resources, Inc.
Made in U.S.A.

The classroom teacher may reproduce copies of materials in this book for classroom use only. The reproduction of any part for an entire school or school system is strictly prohibited. No part of this publication may be transmitted, stored, or recorded in any form without written permission from the publisher.

Table of Contents

Introduction 3	Listening to Native Voices 69
Standards for Writing 4	Writing Across Time 72
Standards Table 5	Windows on Their World 77
Ideas and Content 6	Learning about Each Other 80
Ideas and Content Poster 7	**Organization** 84
Discovering My Great Ideas 8	Organization Poster 85
Exploring My Community 12	From Seeds to Flowers 86
Our Community 15	A Plant's Life 89
My Life in the Community 18	Let's Grow Some Variety 92
Introducing My Community 21	Plant Before You Harvest 95
My Favorite Place 25	Planting a Story 99
Word Choice 28	**Conventions** 104
Word Choice Poster 29	Conventions Poster 105
Animals on Parade 30	The Importance of a Name 106
Our Class Pet 34	All Kinds of People 110
The Night Scamper Came Home 37	One Letter at a Time 113
Listening to Animals 40	Showing the Action 116
Crazy Animals 43	What Is a Paragraph? 119
Fluency 46	**Presentation** 124
Fluency Poster 47	Presentation Poster 125
Playing in the Rain 48	It Takes All Kinds 126
Sunshiny Day 51	Now I See It 130
Seasons of Weather 54	Connecting with My Friend 133
Extreme Weather 58	Help Us Understand You 137
Reporting the Weather 61	Presenting . . . My Friend 140
Voice 64	**Technology Resources** 143
Voice Poster 65	**Answer Key** 144
Many Views of Chenoa 66	

Introduction

In the 1980s, teachers in the Northwest identified several traits, or characteristics, of effective student writing. These traits include Ideas and Content, Word Choice, Fluency, Voice, Organization, and Conventions, and became known as "traits of good writing." Subsequently educators added the trait of Presentation in keeping with state and national standards.

The purpose of this book is to provide teachers with practical, hands-on lesson plans to teach the traits of good writing in the classroom. Each section focuses on one trait, with lessons to teach the trait step-by-step to students. Lessons for each trait include lesson plans, reproducible pages for classroom use, and student samples, or documents, for use in the lessons.

Student samples in each section have a common theme or subject content area. Using themes will help give the lessons cohesiveness in the classroom presentation of each trait and may also assist teachers in incorporating the teaching of trait writing into their daily or weekly teaching schedules. That is, effective writing does not stand alone as something to be practiced in rote exercises but can be incorporated into all facets of student learning.

At the beginning of each section, you will find a poster that highlights the characteristics for the trait. These posters should be enlarged for display and referred to throughout the unit. Many lessons suggest making overhead transparencies or student copies of lesson material, specifically student samples. Teachers may also incorporate this material via scanner into PowerPoint or Smart Board™ presentations for classroom presentation. Students should keep their work in writing folders; many lessons use material students have completed in previous lessons.

Traits of Good Writing

- Ideas and Content
- Word Choice
- Fluency
- Voice
- Organization
- Conventions
- Presentation

Standards for Writing

The following standards are used by permission of McREL (Copyright 2000 MCREL, Mid-continent Research for Education and Learning. Telephone: 303-337-0990. Website: http //www.mcrel.org)

1. Demonstrates competence in the general skills and strategies of the writing process
   A. Prewriting: Uses prewriting strategies to plan written work (e.g., discusses ideas with peers, draws pictures to generate ideas, writes key thoughts and questions, rehearses ideas, records reactions and observations)
   B. Uses graphic organizers, story maps, and webs; groups related ideas; takes notes; brainstorms ideas
   C. Drafting and Revising: Uses strategies to draft and revise written work (e.g., rereads; rearranges words, sentences, and paragraphs to improve or clarify meaning; varies sentence type; adds descriptive words and details; deletes extraneous information; incorporates suggestions from peers and teachers; sharpens the focus)
   D. Elaborates on a central idea; uses paragraphs to develop separate ideas
   E. Editing and Publishing: Uses strategies to edit and publish written work (e.g., proofreads using a dictionary and other resources; edits for grammar, punctuation, capitalization, and spelling at a developmentally appropriate level; incorporates illustrations or photos; shares finished product)
   F. Evaluates own and others' writing (e.g., asks questions and makes comments about writing, helps classmates apply grammatical and mechanical conventions)
   G. Dictates or writes with a logical sequence of events (i.e., includes a beginning, middle, and ending)
   H. Dictates or writes detailed descriptions of familiar persons, places, objects, or experiences
   I. Writes in response to literature
   J. Writes in a variety of formats (e.g., picture books, letters, stories, poems, information pieces)
   K. Writes expressive composition (e.g., expresses ideas, reflections, and observations; uses an individual, authentic voice; uses relevant details; presents ideas that enable a reader to imagine the world of the event or experience)
   L. Writes autobiographical compositions (e.g., provides a context within which the incident occurs, uses simple narrative strategies, provides some insight into why this incident is memorable)
2. Develops awareness of the stylistic and rhetorical aspects of writing (i.e., sentence structure, rhythm)
   A. Uses general, frequently used words to convey basic ideas
   B. Uses descriptive language that clarifies and enhances ideas (e.g., describes familiar people, places, objects)
   C. Uses a variety of sentence structures
3. Uses grammatical and mechanical conventions in written compositions
4. Gathers and uses information for research purposes
   A. Generates questions about topics of personal interest
   B. Uses a variety of strategies to identify topics to investigate (e.g., brainstorms, lists questions, uses idea webs)
   C. Compiles information into oral reports
5. Demonstrates competence in speaking and listening as tools for learning
   A. Makes contributions in class and group discussions (e.g., recounts personal experiences, reports on personal knowledge about a topic, initiates conversations)
   B. Asks and responds to questions
   C. Reads compositions to the class
   D. Organizes ideas for oral presentation (e.g., includes content appropriate to the audience, uses notes or other memory aids, summarizes main points)
   E. Presents simple prepared reports to the class

Standards Table

Lesson	Standard	Page Number
Discovering My Great Ideas	1B	8
Exploring My Community	1A, 1B, 4A, 4B	12
Our Community	1A, 1B, 1C	15
My Life in the Community	1A, 1B, 1H, 1K	18
Introducing My Community	1B, 1E, 1H, 1J, 2B	21
My Favorite Place	1B, 1C, 1E, 1H, 1L	25
Animals on Parade	1B, 2A, 2B	30
Our Class Pet	1B, 1H, 2B, 5D	34
The Night Scamper Came Home	1A, 1C, 1F, 1G, 1J, 2A, 2B	37
Listening to Animals	1H, 1K, 2A, 2B	40
Crazy Animals	1C, 1E, 1J, 5C	43
Playing in the Rain	1B, 1C, 1J, 2B	48
Sunshiny Day	1A, 1E, 1J, 1K, 2B, 5D	51
Seasons of Weather	1C, 1E, 1H, 1J, 2B, 5C	54
Extreme Weather	1A, 1B, 1F, 1G, 2C	58
Reporting the Weather	1B, 1C, 1E, 1F, 1G, 2B, 5B, 5C	61
Many Views of Chenoa	1A, 1I, 1K, 5B	66
Listening to Native Voices	1D, 1J, 1K, 2B, 5A	69
Writing Across Time	1I, 1J, 2A, 5A, 5B	72
Windows on Their World	1C, 1E, 2A, 4B, 4C, 5D, 5E	77
Learning about Each Other	1B, 1C, 1D, 1E, 1F, 1L, 2C	80
From Seeds to Flowers	1A, 1F, 1G, 2A, 5B	86
A Plant's Life	1B, 1C, 1E, 1F, 4B	89
Let's Grow Some Variety	1B, 1D, 1F, 1H, 2C	92
Plant Before You Harvest	1C, 1F, 1G, 2C, 5A, 5B	95
Planting a Story	1B, 1F, 1G, 2C, 5A, 5B	99
The Importance of a Name	1F, 3, 5A	106
All Kinds of People	3	110
One Letter at a Time	1F, 3, 5A, 5B	113
Showing the Action	1A, 3, 5A, 5B	116
What Is a Paragraph?	1C, 1D, 1E, 1F, 3	119
It Takes All Kinds	1A, 1B, 1E, 5B, 5D	126
Now I See It	2A, 4C, 5A, 5B, 5D, 5E	130
Connecting with My Friend	1D, 1H, 1L, 2B, 4A, 5A	133
Help Us Understand You	1B, 1F, 4B, 4C, 5A, 5D	137
Presenting . . . My Friend	1B, 1H, 1J, 2B, 2C, 3, 5C	140

Ideas and Content

This trait lays the foundation for other aspects of effective student writing. Students need to learn to develop and organize their ideas and present them clearly. Students should gather their ideas, as well as research, seek new knowledge, and organize their information, before they begin to write. Successful writers write about what they know, the subjects in which they have expertise, or specific knowledge and experience.

In practicing the characteristics of this trait, students identify topics about which they have prior knowledge, investigate and explore topics further by conducting additional research if needed, and learn to connect their writing to their own experiences.

Writing that is strong in content includes interesting, relevant, specific details and a development of the piece as a whole. Students will practice collecting and organizing their ideas, writing about their own experiences, using examples and details, and writing complete pieces in which they can use insight and understanding to show readers what they know.

Ideas and Content

- gather and organize ideas

- seek new knowledge, explore a topic

- connect writing to your own experience

- use interesting, relevant, specific details

- use clear ideas

- use examples

- show, don't tell

- surprise the reader with what you know

- use insight and understanding

- develop your story, every piece adds to the whole

Ideas and Content Trait

Discovering My Great Ideas

Objective

Given instruction in gathering ideas, students will create a web or other graphic organizer about a specific topic.

Materials

- white board, overhead, or other means of projection
- "Ideas and Content" poster (page 7), one copy for display
- "Community Network" (page 10), one copy for display
- "Learning to Gather Ideas" (page 11), one copy for display and one copy per student

Preparation

Enlarge the "Ideas and Content" poster (page 7) for display. Also enlarge "Community Network" (page 10) and "Learning to Gather Ideas" (page 11) for display.

Opening

Direct the students' attention to the "Ideas and Content" poster (page 7). Introduce the concept of trait writing, telling students they will learn qualities that make their writing more effective and interesting for others to read. Explain that Ideas and Content refers to the process of deciding what to write about and writing in such a way that the reader can easily understand.

Directions

1. Explain to the class that one of the first things authors do before writing is gather information and organize their ideas. Ask students if they know what the term *brainstorm* means. Define if necessary, using a children's dictionary. Ask students how working together to gather ideas might help in their own writing.

2. Display "Community Network" (page 10). Show students how the sample begins with a central topic and branches out to include other related ideas.

3. Display the examples of graphic organizers using "Learning to Gather Ideas" (page 11). Discuss the organizers with the students, explaining how each might be used to gather and organize ideas.

4. Ask students to volunteer specific topic ideas for demonstration. Generate one or two different class graphic organizers using student topic ideas.

Discovering My Great Ideas *(cont.)*

Closing

Review the concept of brainstorming, checking for student understanding. Have students work with a partner to create a graphic organizer (e.g., web, cluster). They should select one of the branches from the class web to use as a starting topic.

Extension

Ask students to select a specific topic related to the community. Have them work individually or in small groups to design a different graphic organizer they could use to gather ideas for this new topic.

Ideas and Content Trait

Community Network
by Holly F.

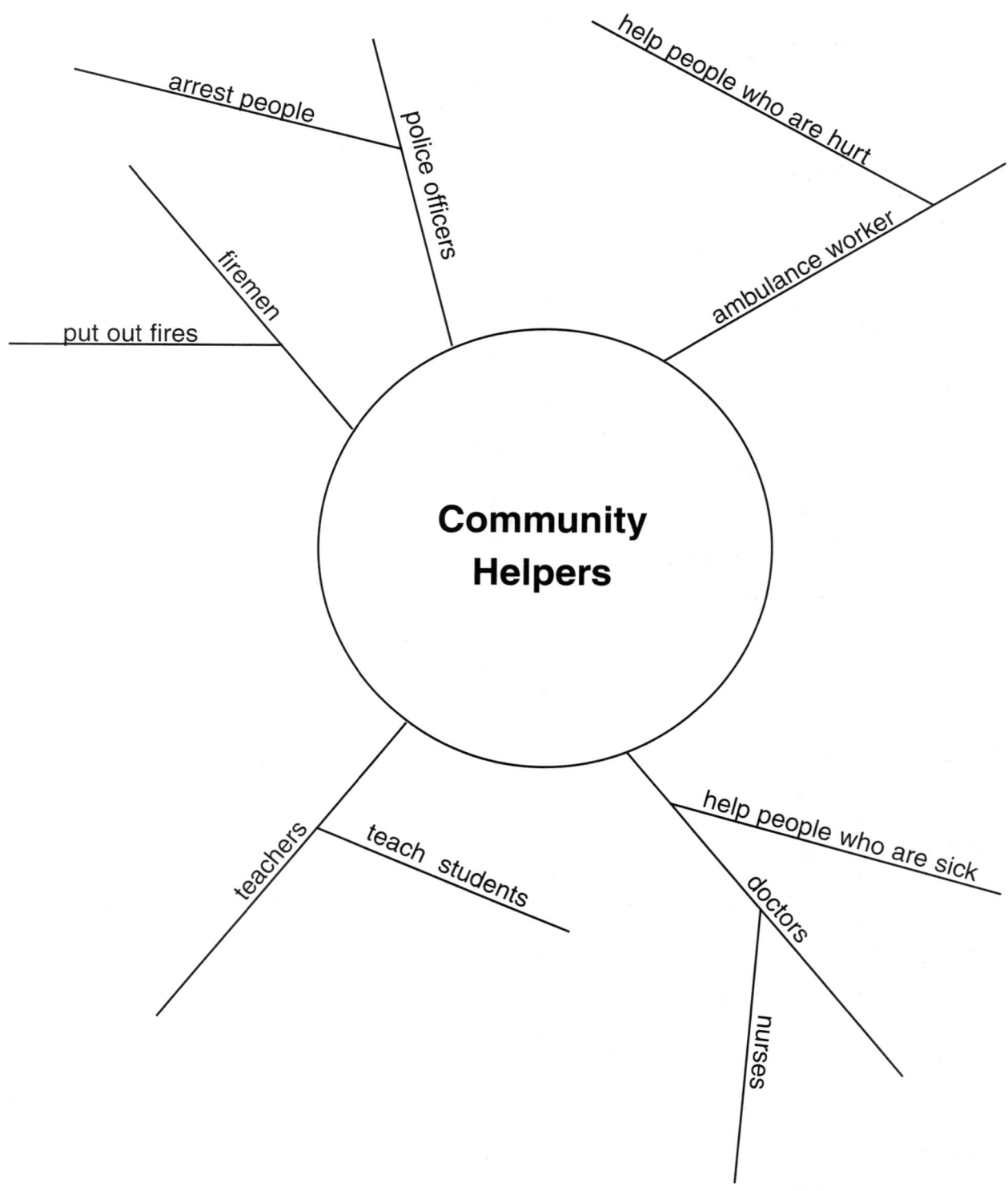

#3584 Traits of Good Writing: Grades 1–2

Ideas and Content Trait

Learning to Gather Ideas

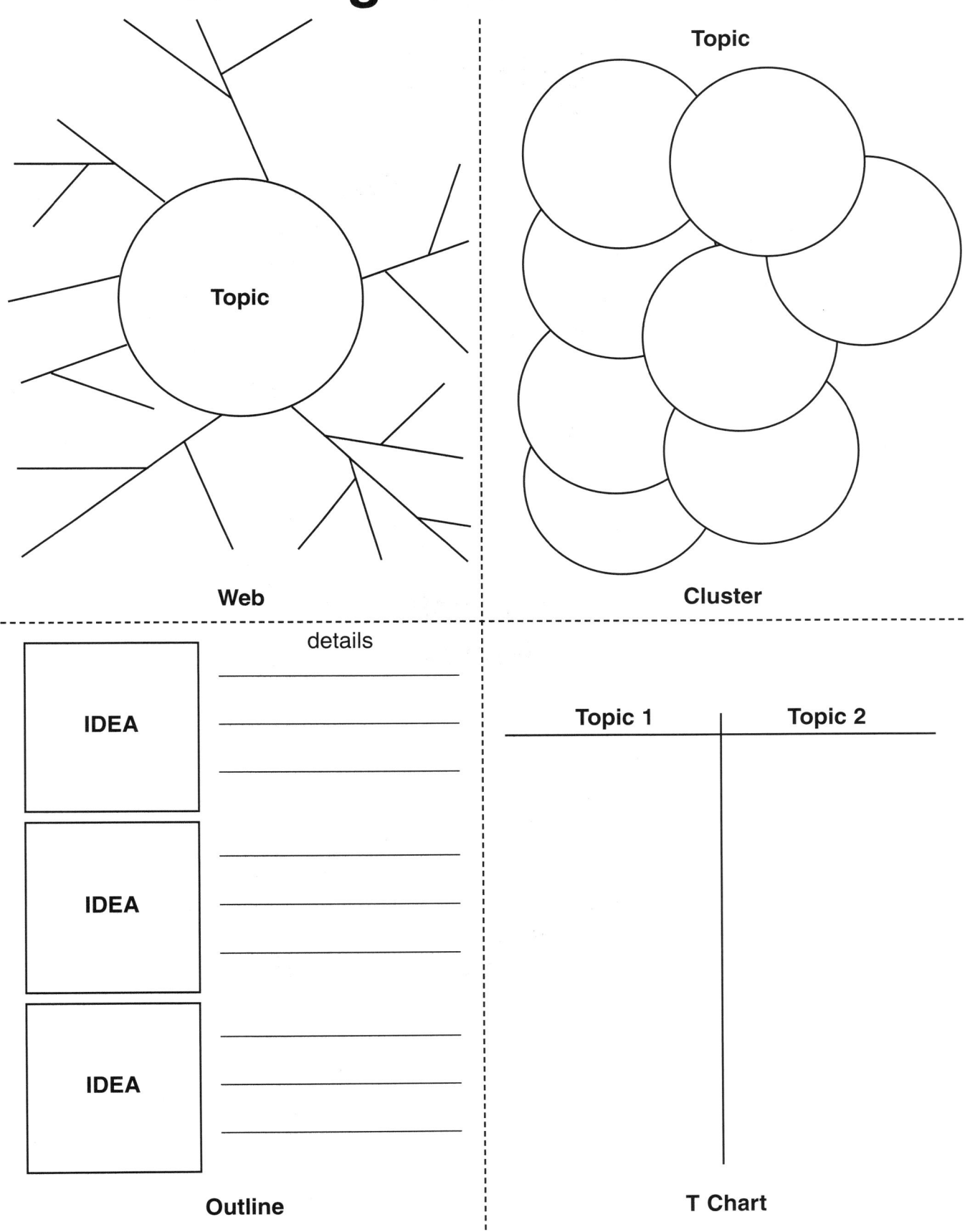

Ideas and Content Trait

Exploring My Community

Objective

Given a definition of research, students will work with others to learn something new about their community.

Materials

- resources about the local community (pamphlets, newspapers, magazines, photographs, brochures, advertisements)
- chart paper, white board, or overhead projector and marker
- colored pencils, crayons, or markers
- "I Learned Something New about My Community" (page 13)
- "My Research Notes" (page 14), one copy per student
- white paper, one sheet per group
- guest speaker to talk about local community (optional)

Opening

Ask students why it might be fun to learn about new places or things. Tell them that anytime they explore and seek new knowledge, they are conducting research. Refer to the "Ideas and Content" poster (page 7) and explain that often writers need to learn more about a topic before they can write effectively.

Directions

1. Continue a class discussion on the meaning of research and exploration, specifically related to writing. Introduce students to the concept of writing new information as they discover it.
2. Demonstrate how to research by showing the class a brochure or pamphlet from the local community. Share specific facts or other points of interest. Model how to take notes using the chart paper.
3. Read "I Learned Something New about My Community" (page 13) to the class. Ask students how they think the author used research to write the paragraph.
4. Explain that students will work with a group to create a map of their community. Divide the class into small groups. Distribute "My Research Notes" (page 14) to each student and one sheet of white paper to each group. They should take notes as they discuss the community within their group, focusing on new things they learn while making the map. Assist students as they work in their groups, clarifying and giving information about the community as needed.

Closing

Have student groups share their maps with the class. Conduct a class discussion, comparing unique features of each group's map.

Extension

Invite a guest speaker from the local community to speak to the class. This person could share facts and other information of interest from his or her specific perspective within the community.

I Learned Something New about My Community

by Faith U.

Kelso was named after Peter Crawford's Scottish home. Kelso was founded in 1884. Kelso is 120 years old. Kelso is the "smelt capital of the world." We came in September 1999. I lived in Kelso for five years. We have new neighbors, a new bridge, and new houses. In the future, there might be a tall building, a lot of new houses, and a dock.

Ideas and Content Trait

My Research Notes

I learned about this new place in our town:

_____
_____
_____
_____

I learned that our town has this store, house of worship, or other building:

_____
_____
_____
_____

I learned more about this interesting place in our community:

_____
_____
_____
_____

I learned about this natural landmark (trees, river, lake, mountain) in our community:

_____
_____

Ideas and Content Trait

Our Community

Objective

Given practice in recognizing details, students will complete a graphic organizer with details and specific examples.

Materials

- white board, overhead projector, or chart paper and colored markers
- photograph of building in the local community
- "This Is My Town" (page 16), one copy for display
- "Features of _____" (page 17), one copy per student
- modeling clay or other materials to build a model (optional)

Preparation

Enlarge "This Is My Town" (page 16) for display.

Opening

Review the points on the "Ideas and Content" poster (page 7) covered thus far. Tell students that in this lesson, they will learn how to include details, clear ideas, and examples in their writing. Show the class a photograph of a specific building in the local community. Ask students to identify details in the picture.

Directions

1. Ask volunteers what it means to include details in writing. A *detail* is a "small part of a whole item, a distinct feature, or specific information about a particular thing." Give examples of details, referring back to the picture displayed in the opening segment.
2. Display a copy of "This Is My Town" (page 16). Read the sample aloud to the class. Have students identify examples of details in the paragraph. Highlight or circle the words with colored markers. Discuss how the author includes clear ideas and examples to help the reader understand the writing.
3. Distribute copies of "Features of _____" (page 17). Have students write the name of their town as part of the title. They will use the graphic organizer to write details about their local community. Students might include specific features of buildings, signs, landmarks, or names of places. Encourage students to consider the five senses as well.

Closing

Have students use page 17 to write a paragraph introducing someone to their community. Remind them to use clear ideas, examples, and details in their writing.

Extension

Divide students into groups. Have them use modeling materials, such as clay, cardboard, plastic containers, wood, and fabric, to make a model of their community. Students should include as many details as possible from their graphic organizers.

This Is My Town

by Tracie H.

My town has many trees on the streets. Some of the trees are towering evergreens, but most are shade trees. On Saturdays I like to ride my bike to the brick library across from the swimming pool. I also like to go to the city park. It has trees, a creek, and a playground with tall swings and a twisting slide. In the summer, the weather gets very hot, but I can always sit under a shady tree.

Ideas and Content Trait

Features of _____

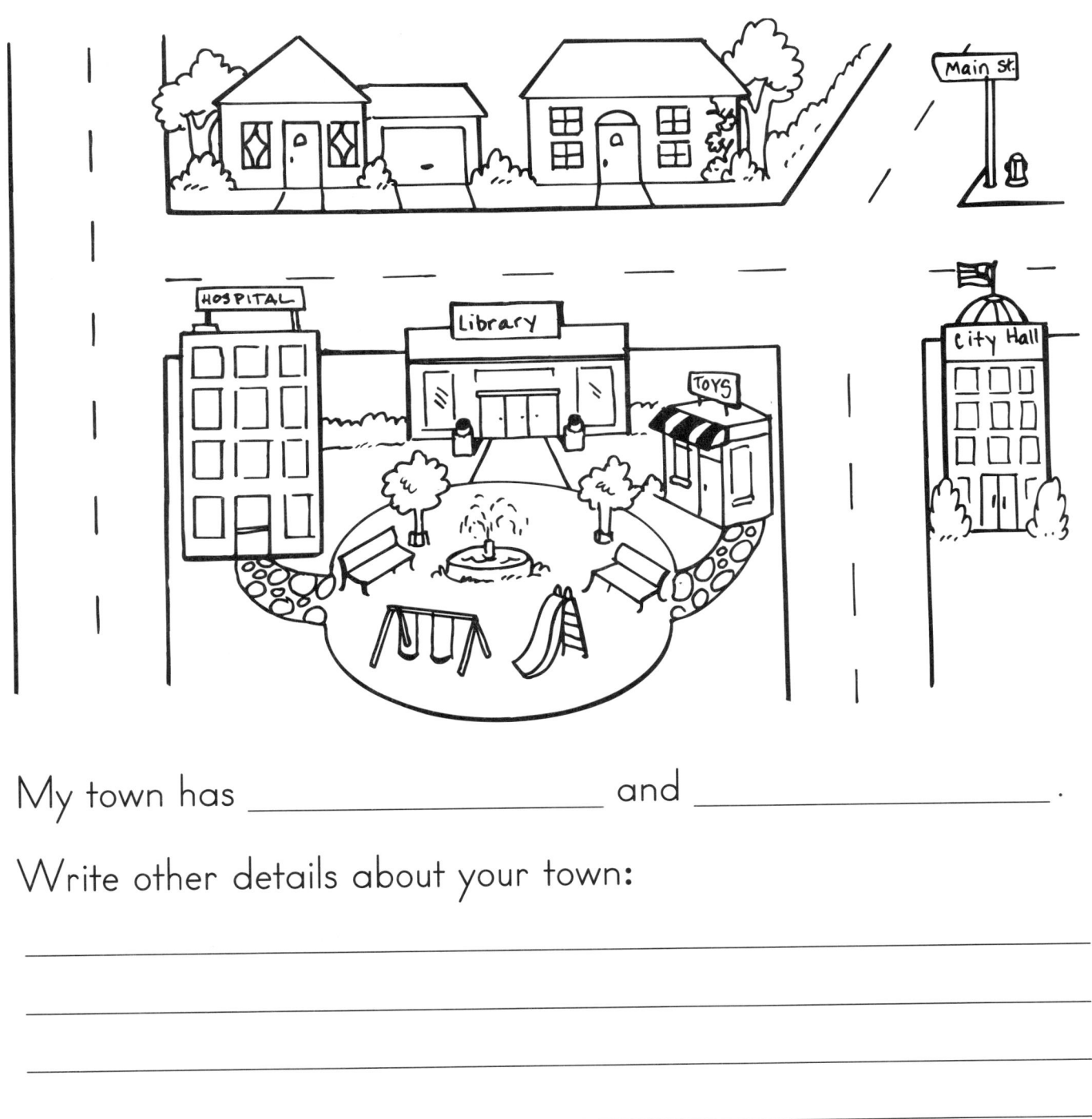

My town has _____ and _____.

Write other details about your town:

_____

_____

_____

_____

Ideas and Content Trait

My Life in the Community

Objective

Given examples of others' experiences and reflections, students will write and illustrate an expressive composition.

Materials

- historical sketches from the local community that would be of interest to students (e.g., student newspapers, information from the library about prominent citizens)
- "My Experiences" (page 19)
- "Making Connections" (page 20), one copy per student

Opening

Ask students to think of stories in which the author wrote about something that happened in his or her life. Discuss examples such as stories by Robert Munsch. Ask students how the author connected his writing to his own life.

Directions

1. Define *experience* and *reflection* for the class, if necessary. Explain that our experiences are the things that happen to us, in this case, in the context of our lives in the community. Discuss the concept of reflection: showing back what the author sees. Give examples from your own life, or ask students to offer examples to demonstrate the concepts of experiences and reflection.
2. Tell students you will read a paragraph to them. Have them listen to discover the writer's thoughts and feelings about his community. Read aloud "My Experiences" (page 19).
3. Distribute copies of "Making Connections" (page 20). Have students write phrases to describe the author's reflections in the mirrors on the top half of the page as you conduct a class discussion about "My Experiences" (page 19).
4. Have students read some of the historical sketches and then use the mirrors on the lower half of the page to write phrases about their thoughts and feelings about their local community.

Closing

Ask students to use the ideas they wrote in the mirrors to write a reflective paragraph about living in their community.

Extension

Photocopy the lower half of the completed "Making Connections" (page 20) for students. Each student trades papers with a partner. Have him or her draw an arrow from the partner's mirrors to a blank area on the page. The student writes how his or her experience compares with the partner's experience. For example, a student writes that he enjoys going to the park with his family, and his partner draws an arrow and writes that she has never been to the park, but she would like to go.

My Experiences

by Jacob B.

I like to go to a resort in Bend. Sometimes there is lightning in the sky. During the day, it is very hot and fun. There are two pools. One has a water slide and a volleyball net. There are four hot tubs with bubbles. White water rafting is exciting and frightening! There are also tennis courts and lots of room to run.

Ideas and Content Trait

Making Connections

Author

Community

Ideas and Content Trait

Introducing My Community

Objective

Given resources and an outline to follow, students will design a brochure that communicates information in a new way.

Materials

- white board, overhead projector, or chart paper and marker
- resources and information about the local community (e.g., community brochures)
- "I Love My World" (page 23), one copy for display
- "A New Look at _____" (page 24), one copy per student
- markers, construction paper or cardstock
- magazine pictures and other art supplies (optional)

Preparation

Enlarge "I Love My World" (page 23) for display.

Opening

Direct students' attention to the "Ideas and Content" poster (page 7) already discussed. Ask students how they could use these skills to present their community in a new and different way to people who live there.

Directions

1. Review the concept that the Ideas and Content trait focuses on how authors present their ideas. Effective writing shows action, rather than telling the reader what happens. Explain that effective writing also surprises the reader with what the author knows and includes insight and understanding about the topic. Including information that might not be obvious to the reader keeps the writing interesting.

2. Show the class the local resources and "I Love My World" (page 23). Allow students time to investigate the content of the materials. Ask what new information they learned about their community and how the authors shared that knowledge. Or read a brochure to the class and discuss it together.

3. Discuss "I Love My World" (page 23). Although this student does not live in your community, as a class determine ways in which the writing exhibits insight and understanding of the author's specific topic (his local community).

4. Distribute copies of "A New Look at _____" (page 24). Tell students they will use this page to gather ideas about how they can write about their town in a new way, including information their reader may not know. Encourage students to be creative and focus on aspects of the community with which they are especially familiar.

Ideas and Content Trait

Introducing My Community (cont.)

Closing

Have students use the ideas generated on the graphic organizer page to create a brochure about their town. They should use color, include details, and work neatly. Brochures may be displayed during a school Open House or at other school or community events.

Extension

Have the class put on a Community Fair. Students may create booths about a particular place in the community related to their brochure. Invite members of another class, parents, or other members of the community to attend the fair. If there are products (e.g., produce, crafts) your community is well known for, these could also be replicated and displayed by the students.

I Love My World

by Caleb V.

The name of my town is La Center. The town was given the name La Center because it was the center of commerce. My town was founded in 1859. My town is 145 years old. The library used to be a hospital. The town was originally named Timmens. Now we have more cows. There are new stores and gas stations. We also have a nice Little League field. In the future, our town might have a new grocery store and possibly a new bank.

Ideas and Content Trait

A New Look at _____

Our town might get a new . . .
_____

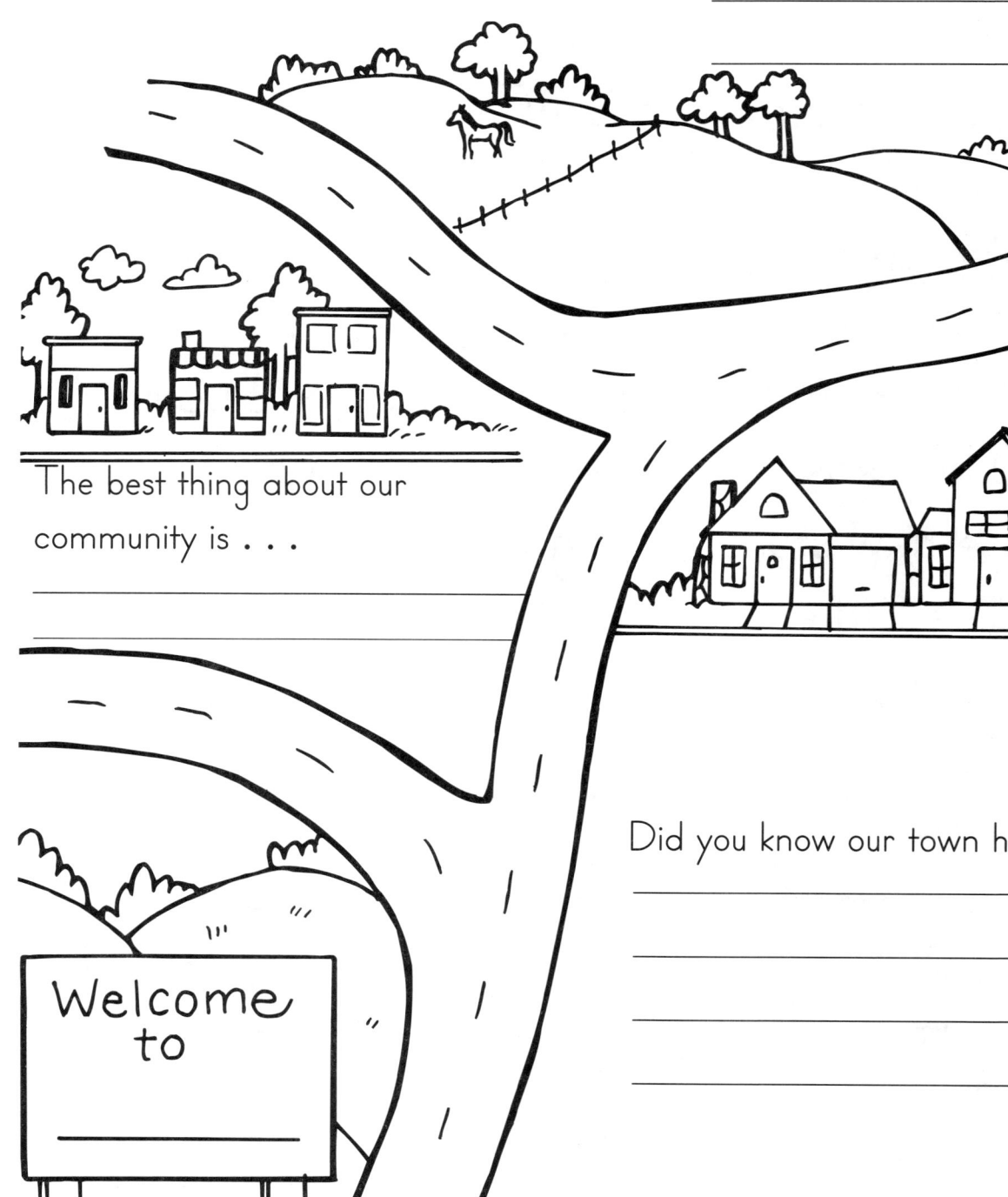

The best thing about our community is . . .
_____

Welcome to _____

Did you know our town has . . .
_____
_____
_____

Ideas and Content Trait

My Favorite Place

Objective

Given a familiar topic and an outline, students will develop a complete piece of writing using the characteristics of the Ideas and Content trait.

Materials

- resources (maps, pictures, etc.) from the local community used in previous lessons
- "Frozen Fun" (page 26), one copy per student
- colored pencils
- "Places I Like to Go" (page 27), one copy per student

Opening

Review with the students the "Ideas and Content" poster (page 7). Explain that as writers incorporate these characteristics into their writing, they will develop their story. Every word and sentence should contribute to the entire piece; if a phrase does not add to the author's story, the author should remove it.

Directions

1. Remind students that as they write from their own experiences, it becomes especially important to make sure that every sentence adds to the story. When writing about their own life, authors should take care not to include extra information. At the same time, students will need to include details, examples, and new information to keep their writing interesting to the reader.
2. Distribute copies of "Frozen Fun" (page 26). As a class, work together to identify details, new information, or phrases that especially add to the piece. Have students use different colors to mark each aspect you discuss.
3. Tell students they will also write about their favorite place in the community. Distribute copies of "Places I Like to Go" (page 27). Have students complete the page to gather ideas about their favorite places. Students should choose one place to write about. Encourage students to use descriptive words and include details.

Closing

Ask students to write a paragraph about their favorite place in the community. Allow students time to edit their work and produce a final copy. Students' pieces about favorite places may be bound into a class book or shared in another way with parents and members of the community.

Extension

Have students use their idea pages to create advertising posters, depicting their favorite place. Display the posters around the classroom, in the library or hallway, or around the community.

Ideas and Content Trait

Frozen Fun

by Shayla X.

Woo hoo! Today I get to go to Frozen Fun Ice Cream! I enjoy the ice cream there. The people who work there are kind. My mom told me we could not go today! I was so upset. I begged and begged and begged. Finally, we got to go. I always get vanilla ice cream with rainbow sprinkles and white chocolate chips on it. I treasure Frozen Fun Ice Cream!

Ideas and Content Trait

Places I Like to Go

My favorite place in my community is . . .
_____
_____

It looks like . . .
_____
_____

I like it because . . .
_____
_____

It has . . .
_____
_____

I go there with . . .
_____
_____

This place is special to me because . . .
_____
_____

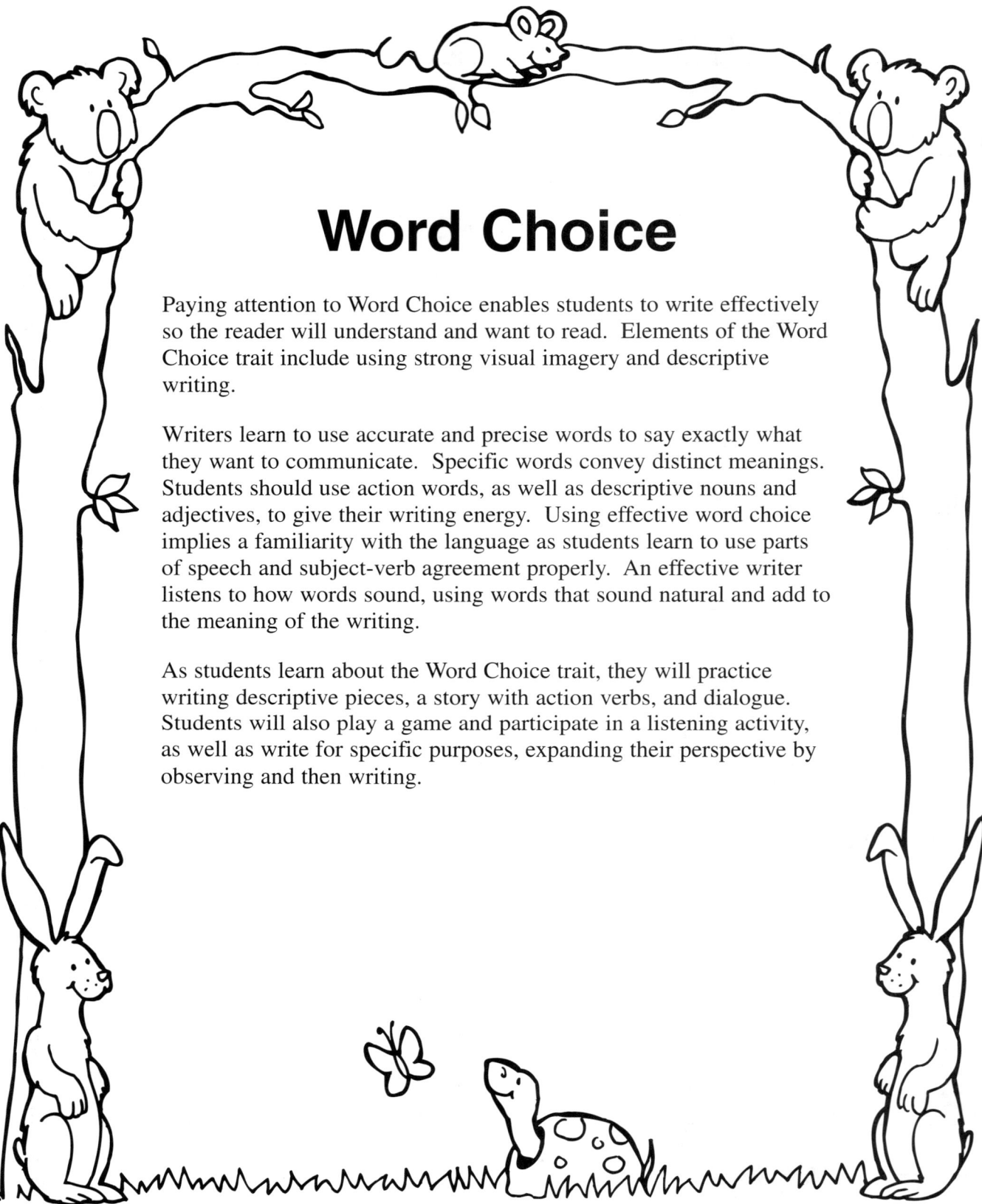

Word Choice

Paying attention to Word Choice enables students to write effectively so the reader will understand and want to read. Elements of the Word Choice trait include using strong visual imagery and descriptive writing.

Writers learn to use accurate and precise words to say exactly what they want to communicate. Specific words convey distinct meanings. Students should use action words, as well as descriptive nouns and adjectives, to give their writing energy. Using effective word choice implies a familiarity with the language as students learn to use parts of speech and subject-verb agreement properly. An effective writer listens to how words sound, using words that sound natural and add to the meaning of the writing.

As students learn about the Word Choice trait, they will practice writing descriptive pieces, a story with action verbs, and dialogue. Students will also play a game and participate in a listening activity, as well as write for specific purposes, expanding their perspective by observing and then writing.

Word Choice

- write with descriptive words

- use strong visual imagery

- use accurate and precise words to convey a specific meaning

- understand that action verbs give writing energy

- be familiar with language

- use words that sound natural

- listen to how words sound, adding to the meaning of the writing

Word Choice Trait

Animals on Parade

Objective
Given instruction about the parts of speech, students will identify descriptive words and play a game.

Materials
- white board, overhead projector, or chart paper and marker
- poster board or chart paper to display cards
- "Word Choice" poster (page 29), one copy for display
- "In the Zoo" (page 31), one copy per student
- Zoo Game Cards (pages 32–33), one set per group
- index cards or sticky notes
- cardstock

Preparation
Enlarge the "Word Choice" poster (page 29) for display. Photocopy the Zoo Game Cards (pages 32–33) onto cardstock and laminate if desired. Cut out the cards.

Opening
Show students the "Word Choice" poster (page 29). Explain that in order to choose effective words and use descriptive words in writing, a writer must be familiar with the types of words in our language.

Directions
1. Define *noun*, *verb*, and *adjective*. Hold a class discussion, asking students to give examples of each type of word (e.g., nouns in and around the school, actions people do during the day, descriptions of specific objects or places).
2. Divide the class into small groups. Distribute to each group a set of Zoo Game Cards (pages 32–33). Have students sort the cards into nouns, verbs, and adjectives, and place the cards under the correct heading on a poster to form a word bank.
3. Distribute copies of "In the Zoo" (page 31). Ask students to add their own nouns, verbs, and adjectives to the organizer in the appropriate spaces. Monitor students as they work, checking for understanding and correct placement of words.

Closing
Have students share their most creative descriptive words (e.g., nouns, verbs, adjectives) from page 31. Add these words to the class word bank.

Extension
Play the game, Going to the Zoo. Divide students into groups. Give each group one set of Zoo Game Cards. Tell students that the object of the game is to collect sets of cards. (The game is played like "Go Fish".) A set may consist of one noun card, one verb card, and one adjective card, or three of a kind. Three of a kind is worth five points, one of each is worth 10 points.

Word Choice Trait

In the Zoo

Nouns _____

Verbs _____

Adjectives _____

Word Choice Trait

Zoo Game Cards

monkey	nest
bucket	blanket
seeds	lunch
twig	doctor
climb	clean
fly	sweep

Zoo Game Cards (cont.)

eat	jump
play	run
loud	fast
tiny	green
warm	fluffy
crunchy	wet

Word Choice Trait

Our Class Pet

Objective

Given a stuffed animal to observe, students will complete a graphic organizer using words to convey visual imagery and write a paragraph.

Materials

- stuffed animal(s)
- "My Dog" (page 35)
- "Introducing Our Pet" (page 36), one copy per student
- animal border, cutouts, and other decorative items (optional)

Opening

Read "My Dog" (page 35) aloud. Then ask students if they have a picture in their minds of the animal about which you just read. Ask students to identify which words in the paragraph helped them "see" the animal. Write the words on the board. Explain that these words create visual imagery; they help readers see in their minds what the author sees.

Directions

1. Introduce the classroom stuffed animal(s) for observation. Invite students to help you name the animal(s). Tell the class they will need to observe the animal closely so they will be able to describe the animal to someone who has not seen it.
2. Distribute copies of "Introducing Our Pet" (page 36). Go over the graphic organizer with students, explaining and defining each part as necessary.
3. Have students complete the graphic organizer using the classroom stuffed animal as a model. Tell them they should carefully look at the animal as they describe it, and they should imagine how the animal might act, move, smell, and sound if it was alive.

Closing

If you have more than one stuffed animal on display, have each student introduce the animal he or she selected to a partner. If students observed the same animal, have the class visit another class and introduce the animal to a younger student. Remind your students to use visual imagery to describe the animal to someone who has not seen it.

Extension

Have students use the information on page 36 to write a paragraph about the classroom animal(s). Display student work on a bulletin board. If possible, include photographs of the stuffed animal in the bulletin board display.

My Dog

by Faith U.

My dog is small and fat for his size. He is very cute. He has little teeth. His fur is black and brown. His skin color is tan and a little lighter than ours.

Word Choice Trait

Introducing Our Pet

This is how our class pet looks . . .
_____
_____
_____

Our class pet makes these sounds . . .
_____
_____
_____

Our class pet feels . . .
_____
_____
_____

Our class pet eats . . .
_____
_____
_____

This is how our class pet moves . . .
_____
_____
_____

Word Choice Trait

The Night Scamper Came Home

Objective

Given instruction on types of verbs and the opportunity to observe a stuffed animal, students will imagine, write about, and illustrate possible activities with an animal guest.

Materials

- poster board, chart paper, or other place to display cards
- stuffed animal(s) (from "Our Class Pet" on page 34)
- "Animal Antics" (page 39), one copy for display and one per student
- "Caleb and Monkey Boy" (page 38), one copy per student
- colored pencils
- pictures of people doing something: thinking, feeling, and talking (optional)

Preparation

Enlarge "Animal Antics" (page 39) for display.

Opening

Draw students' attention to the "Word Choice" poster (page 29). Ask students to identify and review aspects of the trait studied thus far.

Directions

1. Discuss and define the term *action verbs*. Tell students that verbs are "words that show action," but there are also other kinds of verbs. Display a copy of "Animal Antics" (page 39). Define each type of verb, asking students for examples of each. Show sample pictures if available.
2. Distribute copies of "Caleb and Monkey Boy" (page 38). Work together as a class to read the story and circle the verbs using colored pencils.
3. Distribute copies of "Animal Antics" (page 39). Tell students they should write ideas of what they would do with the stuffed animal if it came home with them for one night.

Closing

Have students use page 39 to write a story about their visit with the stuffed animal. Encourage students to use dialogue; tell them they might talk with the animal and it might answer back. The students can write what each character says.

Extension

Ask students to write a letter to you about their adventures with the stuffed animal. Or have students work in small groups to write a skit about the stuffed animal's adventures with them. Groups may present their skits to the rest of the class.

Word Choice Trait

Caleb and Monkey Boy

by Caleb V.

His name will be Monkey Boy. When I get home, we will play jump rope. I will see if he can jump on my shoulder and eat a banana. We will see who can get to the trash can first. Then we will go outside and go on the rope swing and climb trees.

We will play hide and go seek. Monkey Boy likes to hide in trees. He goes in trees when we play tag so I can't get him. Then I will watch him do tricks like back flips and cartwheels. He's a good performer.

Then we will get a tent and think of funny or scary stories. Then we will go to sleep.

Then we will go back to school. I will ask if I can keep Monkey Boy!

Word Choice Trait

Animal Antics

Speaking Verbs 	Thinking Verbs 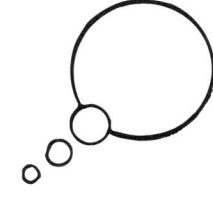
Feeling Verbs 	Acting Verbs 

Word Choice Trait

Listening to Animals

Objectives

Given a listening experience, students will draw a picture of the animal described. Given a picture to color, students will write a short paragraph for a partner.

Materials

- "Animal Sounds" (page 41)
- sample paragraph (page 41)
- colored pencils or crayons
- "Animal Details" (page 42), one copy per student (optional)

Opening

Review with students the concepts of visual and auditory imagery. Tell them that the way some words sound helps the reader understand what the author is trying to say.

Directions

1. Read several "sound" words to the class (see "Animal Sounds" on page 41). Ask them what images they think of when they hear these words.

2. Define *accurate* or *precise* for the students. Tell them that using precise words means that a writer chooses exactly the right word to convey what he or she wants to say. Ask students to identify the most accurate word in examples: Would you describe a big house as a mansion or a cottage? If someone is talking quietly, are they whispering or yelling? Offer other examples as well.

3. Tell the class they will need to carefully listen for words that describe an animal as you read a paragraph to them. Read the sample paragraph on page 41. The students should draw a color picture of the animal described in the paragraph.

Closing

Display student pictures in such a way that everyone in the class can see them. (You may wish to post drawings anonymously.) Read the sample paragraph (page 41) again, and ask students which pictures most accurately portray the animal described.

Extension

Distribute copies of "Animal Details" (page 42). Have students color the page. Ask them to write a paragraph describing their picture. Display pictures and paragraphs and have students guess which classmate completed which picture.

Word Choice Trait

Animal Sounds

bark	purr	scream
scratch	whistle	hiss
growl	oink	screech
wag	meow	moo

Sample Paragraph
Faith U.

The dog barks a lot. If you scare him, he'll bite and scratch you. Sometimes he will play with you and wag his tail while he plays. He growls when he is mad. When he is tired he will cuddle with you. Sometimes he even protects you.

Word Choice Trait

Animal Details

Word Choice Trait

Crazy Animals

Objective
Given a review of the characteristics of the Word Choice trait (page 29), students will demonstrate familiarity with descriptive language by making a strip book.

Materials
- puppets
- Sample Strip Book (page 44)
- "My Funny Animal Story" (page 45), two copies per student and two copies for Sample Strip Book
- colored construction paper, 9" x 12" (23 cm x 30 cm), one sheet per student and one sheet for Sample Strip Book
- scissors and stapler
- markers or crayons

Preparation
Use two copies of page 45 to create a Sample Strip Book. Fold the paper along the solid line. Cut between the words along the dashed lines to create strips. (Do not cut all the way to the fold). Place the folded pages inside a folded construction-paper cover. Staple the booklet.

Opening
Focus students' attention on the "Word Choice" poster (page 29). Ask students to review the concepts of precise words and using words that sound natural. You might want to read a couple of brief examples from picture books to review these concepts.

Directions
1. Use puppets to demonstrate how someone who is familiar with our language would speak. Use another puppet to demonstrate someone speaking who is not familiar with our language. Ask students to identify the differences between the two puppets. Talk with the class about being familiar with the language: they listen to people speak from the time they are born and they learn to speak the language themselves by hearing it spoken. Each year they learn new words, meanings, and how to read, write, and speak so other people can better understand what they are trying to say.

2. Show the class the completed Sample Strip Book. Explain that the book is folded between a construction-paper cover, and each page is cut into strips. Demonstrate how the strips can be moved to create different stories.

3. Distribute copies of "My Funny Animal Story" (page 45) and construction paper to students. Remind students to use precise, descriptive words. Tell students to fold the "My Funny Animal Story" pages in half (along the solid line). Demonstrate how to cut the pages into strips (but not all the way to the fold). Students should place their folded pages inside a folded construction-paper cover. Staple the booklets.

Word Choice Trait

Crazy Animals (cont.)

Directions (cont.)

4. Have students write an adjective in the first strip on the page, a noun in the second strip, a verb in the third strip, and an adverb in the fourth strip. Tell students an adverb tells how or when something happened.

Closing

Have the students decorate the cover of their booklets. Instruct the students to read aloud their book to a small group and then take it home to share with their families.

Extension

Students may place their strip books in the classroom or school library. You might also arrange for them to share their books with another class.

Sample Strip Book

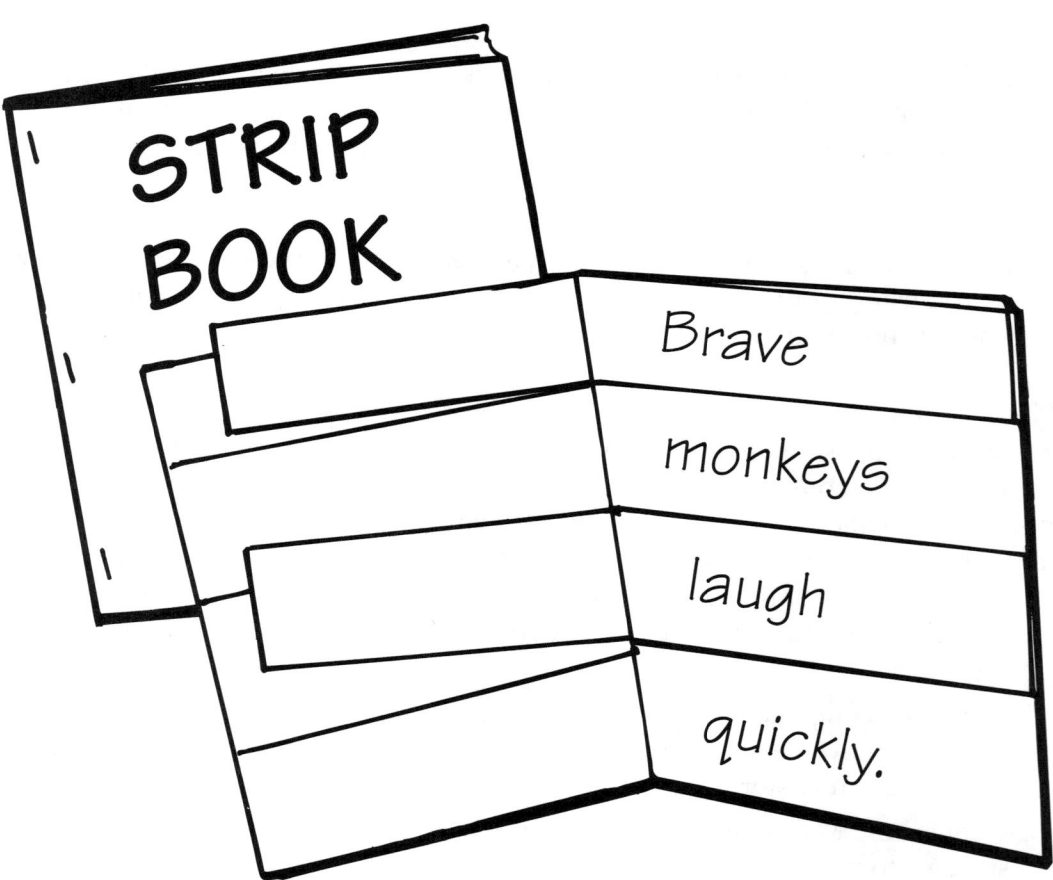

Word Choice Trait

My Funny Animal Story

Fluency

As students learn to incorporate the trait of Fluency in their writing, they continue their exploration of language, begun during the study of the Word Choice trait. As writers develop fluency, they play with different word patterns and use words to match the mood of their writing. Fluent writing contains sentences varying in length and structure.

Students should learn to express themselves in clear sentences that make sense. This will happen as they incorporate natural rhythm and flow in their writing, making sure that ideas begin purposefully and connect to one another. A writer may engage in a process of thinking that begins by asking the question, "What if?" One question leads to another, and the writer begins to develop smooth transitions and pacing. Each component of the Fluency trait contributes to a final characteristic: effective writing will pass a "read-aloud" test.

As students learn about the Fluency trait, they will practice writing in a variety of formats. They will gather words to create word patterns and match specific moods. Students will also evaluate one another, reviewing traits studied thus far as they participate in read-aloud activities.

Fluency

- play with language and words
- use different word patterns
- use appropiate words to match the mood of the piece
- vary sentence length and structure
- write clear sentences that make sense
- write with natural rhythm and flow
- use the process of thinking, "What if?"
- make sure ideas begin purposefully and connect to one another
- try the "read-aloud" test

Fluency Trait

Playing in the Rain

Objective

Given an experience watching a puppet skit, students will apply information about word patterns to create short rhymes.

Materials

- white board, overhead projector, or chart paper and marker
- "Fluency" poster (page 47), one copy for display
- puppets, puppet stage
- "When It Rains, Make Your Own Sunshine" (page 49), copies for volunteer puppeteers
- "Just Playing Around" (page 50), one copy per student
- props for puppet skit as identified in script (optional)

Preparation

Enlarge the "Fluency" poster (page 47) for display. Enlist the help of volunteers (students, parents, or other adults) to present the puppet skit. Give them copies of "When It Rains, Make Your Own Sunshine" (page 49) and allow time for practice. If commercial puppets are not available, make simple puppets using clean white socks and felt tip markers. Draw the puppet's face on the foot of the sock and add other decorations, such as hair, as desired.

Opening

Share with students the "Fluency" poster (page 47). Explain that authors use their familiarity with language to experiment with patterns and words to match the mood of a written piece.

Directions

1. Tell students they will watch a puppet skit. Ask them to notice and identify ways in which the puppet characters play with words and language. Have students also listen for word patterns. Have volunteers present the puppet skit to the class.
2. Conduct a class discussion about the skit. Ask students to identify word play they observed in the skit.
3. Distribute copies of "Just Playing Around" (page 50). Have students color the pictures. After they color, they will write words on the lines to create short rhymes.

Closing

Ask student volunteers to review for the class the concepts of playing with language, word play, and word patterns. You might have small groups teach each concept to their peers in a mini-lesson format.

Extension

Have students use the rhymes and rhythms they wrote on page 50 to write jump rope rhymes. Have them teach their jump rope rhymes to classmates. Take the class outside and allow time to jump rope using the new rhymes.

When It Rains, Make Your Own Sunshine

by Caleb V. and Faith U.

Katie: I am so bored. There is nothing to do.
Jack: Let's get hot chocolate and blankets and slippers and sit by the fireplace and read books.
Katie: Ok, we can also tell jokes.
Jack: I have one for you. What does the Sun like to eat?
Katie: What?
Jack: Sunchips!
Katie: Ok, here's one. What does rain like to make?
Jack: I don't know, raindrops?
Katie: No, rainbows. What does the Sun like to make?
Jack: Sunbows?
Katie: A sunrise!
Jack: What is the Sun's favorite day of the week?
Katie: Sunday?
Jack: Yes, you got it! What does rain like to eat?
Katie: I don't know, what?
Jack: Gummy raindrops!
Katie: Hey, look, it stopped raining!
Jack: All right! Let's go splash in mud puddles!
The puppets dance offstage with boots and raincoats on.

Fluency Trait

Just Playing Around

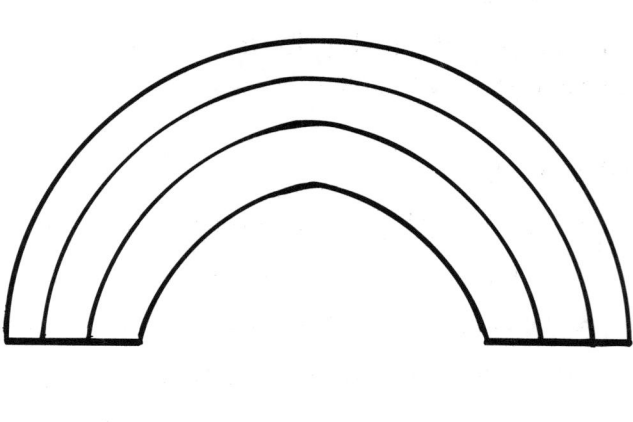

_____
_____
_____

_____
_____
_____

_____
_____
_____
_____

Fluency Trait

Sunshiny Day

Objective

Given a class discussion about different types of weather, students will use appropriate words to match a specific mood to create a poster.

Materials

- white board, overhead projector, or chart paper and marker
- pictures of different types of weather and other weather-related resources
- "A Dreary Gray Day" (page 52), one copy per student
- "Perfect Weather" (page 53), one copy per student
- 8½" x 11" (21.5 cm x 28 cm) cardstock, one sheet per student
- markers and rulers

Opening

Show students pictures of different types of weather. Ask students how the pictures make them feel. What type of weather makes them feel happy? sad? excited? afraid? uncertain? Explain that *mood* refers not only to how someone feels, but also to that person's attitude or general outlook on life at the moment.

Directions

1. Review with students the concept that fluent writing includes appropriate words to match the mood. Refer to the pictures again and ask students to give words to describe the mood of each picture. Write the words on the white board.
2. Distribute copies of "A Dreary Gray Day" (page 52). Discuss the words the author used in his writing. Ask students how effectively the chosen words convey the intended mood. You might want to have students offer more appropriate words.
3. Distribute copies of "Perfect Weather" (page 53). Tell the class they will create a poster highlighting a specific type of weather. Have students use this page to plan their poster. Encourage students to use appropriate words to convey the mood of their weather topic. Students may refer to the copy of "Dreary Gray Day" (page 52) for appropriate word choices.

Closing

Distribute poster board, markers, and other supplies for students to make posters. The students should use "Perfect Weather" (page 53) as a planning guide as they work.

Extension

Students may use page 53 and the weather-related pictures and resources to create a travel brochure advertising a specific place that has their chosen type of weather.

Fluency Trait

A Dreary Gray Day

by Julian A.

My favorite weather is snow. When it snows, you can ride on sleds. If the snow stacks up high enough, you can go really fast. In the snow you can surprise your neighbors with snowballs.

Fluency Trait

Perfect Weather

My poster will be about:

☐ rain ☐ snow

☐ sunshine ☐ wind or fog

The writing will say:
_____
_____
_____

The pictures will be of:
_____ _____
_____ _____
_____ _____

I will decorate my page with:

☐ a border

☐ different types of lines or boxes

☐ fancy letters

Draw a picture in the box to show where you will put words and pictures on your poster.

Fluency Trait

Seasons of Weather

Objective

Given instruction in format and types of complete sentences, students will write two to three sentences for each season.

Materials

- "Fall, Winter, Spring, Summer" (page 56), one copy for sample wheel
- "A Year of Weather" (page 57), one copy per student
- colored construction paper, 9" x 12" (23 cm x 30 cm), one sheet per student
- brads, scissors
- pictures of the different seasons (optional)

Preparation

Cut a construction-paper cover for the wheel (page 56) and fasten it with a brad in the center. Cut out a window so students can view one section at a time. If desired, photocopy a large circle pattern onto construction paper for your students to cut the covers for their wheels.

Opening

Review with students the "Fluency" poster (page 47). Discuss the aspects of rhythm, flow, words to match a mood, and word patterns, and relate these features to the seasons of the year. You might want to show students pictures of the different seasons or refer to classroom pictures and art, depicting different aspects of weather and seasons of the year.

Directions

1. Introduce students to the concept of varied sentence length and structure. Teach the class the three basic types of sentences: statement, question, and exclamation. Review with students the components of a complete sentence: beginning capital, ending punctuation, noun and verb, and the sentence should make sense. Demonstrate with sample sentences, if necessary.

2. Explain that authors can vary their sentences by using one or more types of sentences in their writing. Emphasize that sentences must be clear and make sense to the reader.

3. Continue the discussion by showing the class the sample wheel (see Preparation) and sentences. Ask students to state the types of sentences used and how the sentences make sense.

4. Tell students they will also make a wheel of seasons. Distribute copies of "A Year of Weather" (page 57). Use the sample wheel (page 56) to demonstrate how to write sentences on the wheel, cut it out, make a cover, and assemble the wheel with a brad.

Seasons of Weather (cont.)

Directions (cont.)

5. Have students write two to three sentences for each season on the appropriate section of the wheel. Monitor and assist students as they write their sentences, cut out the wheel and cover, and assemble the booklets.

Closing

Have students decorate the cover of their wheel booklets. Ask students to share their booklet with a partner. Have students check their partners' sentences for clarity.

Extension

Use a classroom weather graph to predict the next three days' weather. Have students write a weather forecast following a format used in the newspaper or TV news. Discuss with the class how the weather appears to follow patterns. Weather forecasters often use different sentences to hold a reader's interest while describing similar types of weather. Students may compare their forecasts and take note of word patterns and variety in sentence structure.

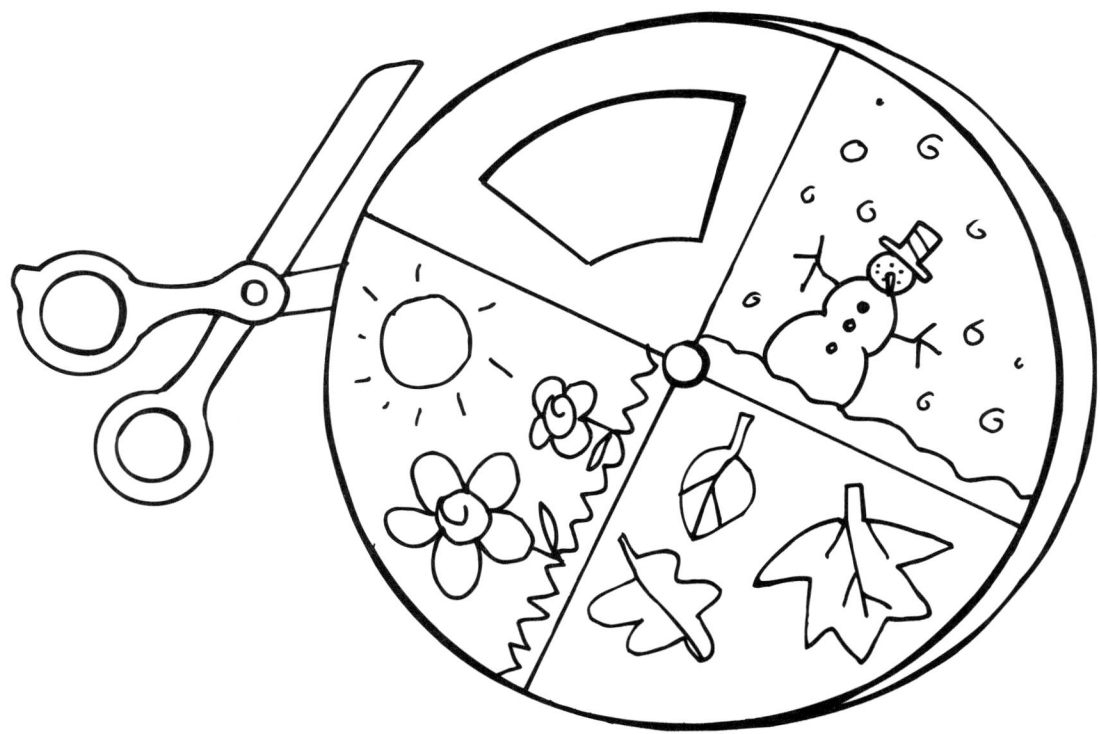

Fluency Trait

Fall, Winter, Spring, Summer

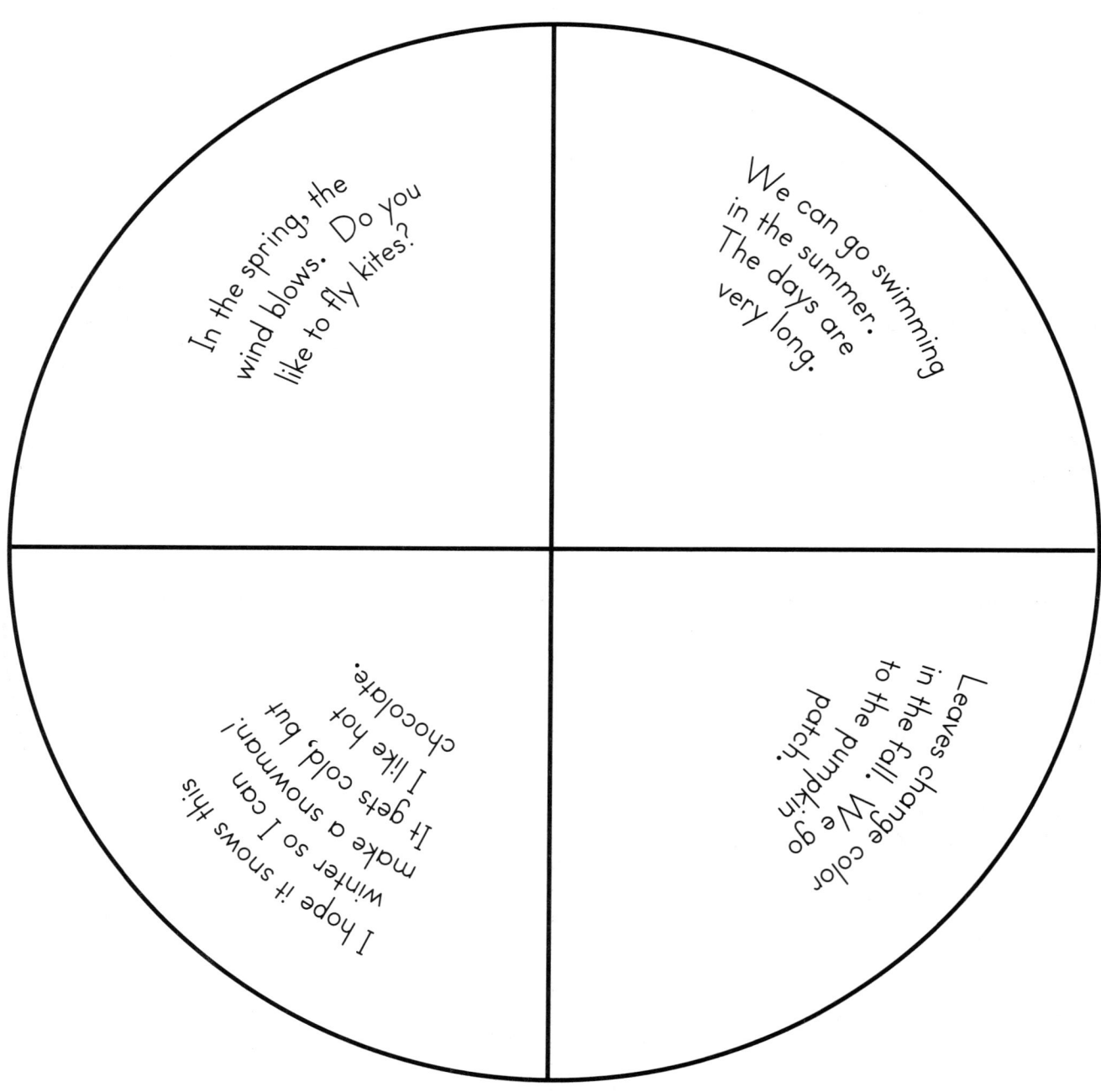

Fluency Trait

A Year of Weather

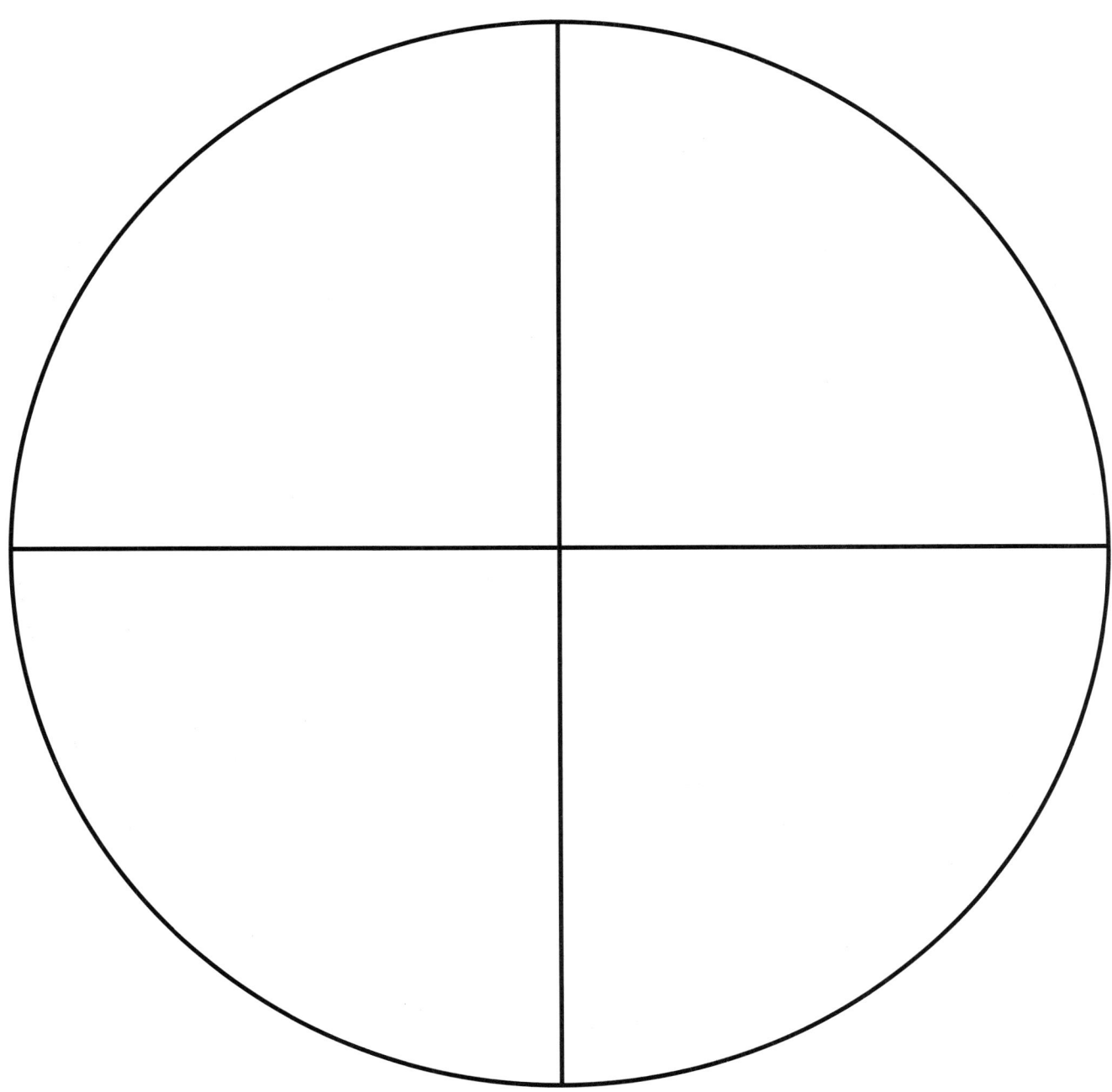

Fluency Trait

Extreme Weather

Objective
Given a review of the characteristics of the Fluency trait, students will write sentences with connecting ideas.

Materials
- poster board, chart paper, or other place to display cards
- a connecting story such as *The House That Jack Built* or *Curious George* (H.A. Rey)
- weather-related resources used in previous lessons
- "What If Lightning Struck?" (page 59), one copy for display
- arrow patterns (page 96)
- thumbtacks or tape
- "Sunshine to Snowstorm" (page 60), one copy per student

Preparation
Enlarge "What If Lightning Struck?" (page 59) and the arrow patterns (page 96) for display. Cut out the arrows.

Opening
Read a picture book to the class. Ask students how each idea in the story connects to the next idea. Draw students' attention to the "Fluency" poster (page 47), focusing on "make sure ideas begin purposefully and connect to one another."

Directions
1. Tell students that as writers work, they consider what would happen next in the story if a particular thing happened. Give examples from the book you read.

2. Display "What If Lightning Struck?" (page 59). Have the students place arrows, using thumbtacks, where ideas connect in the story.

3. Have students create a class story: Give students a starting sentence such as "One day I saw some very dark, strange clouds unlike any I had ever seen before." Call on a volunteer to tell what might happen next in the story. Repeat with several students until the class has reached a possible ending for the story. If you wish, write the story on the overhead projector as the students dictate their sentences.

4. Distribute copies of "Sunshine to Snowstorm" (page 60) to the class. Explain that students should write about one type of weather and what that weather might lead to. For example, if there are clouds in the sky, it might rain. Encourage students to use weather resources for ideas about unusual types of weather and what causes different types of weather.

Fluency Trait

Extreme Weather *(cont.)*

Closing

Have students use page 60 to write a story about extreme weather. Tell them that they should ask themselves "What would happen if . . . ?" often as they write the story.

Extension

Have each student use page 60 to write a letter to a relative. The students should use their imaginations to predict what might happen if they were caught in extreme weather.

What If Lightning Struck?
by Caleb V.

If I was running and lightning struck, I would run and jump to get under something safe.

If it was my brother who heard lightning, he'd jump out and run around and probably get shocked.

Once the lightning stopped, I'd run from the turkey to the house.

My brother would get shocked and the turkey would peck him.

Then he would probably make it to the house.

Fluency Trait

Sunshine to Snowstorm

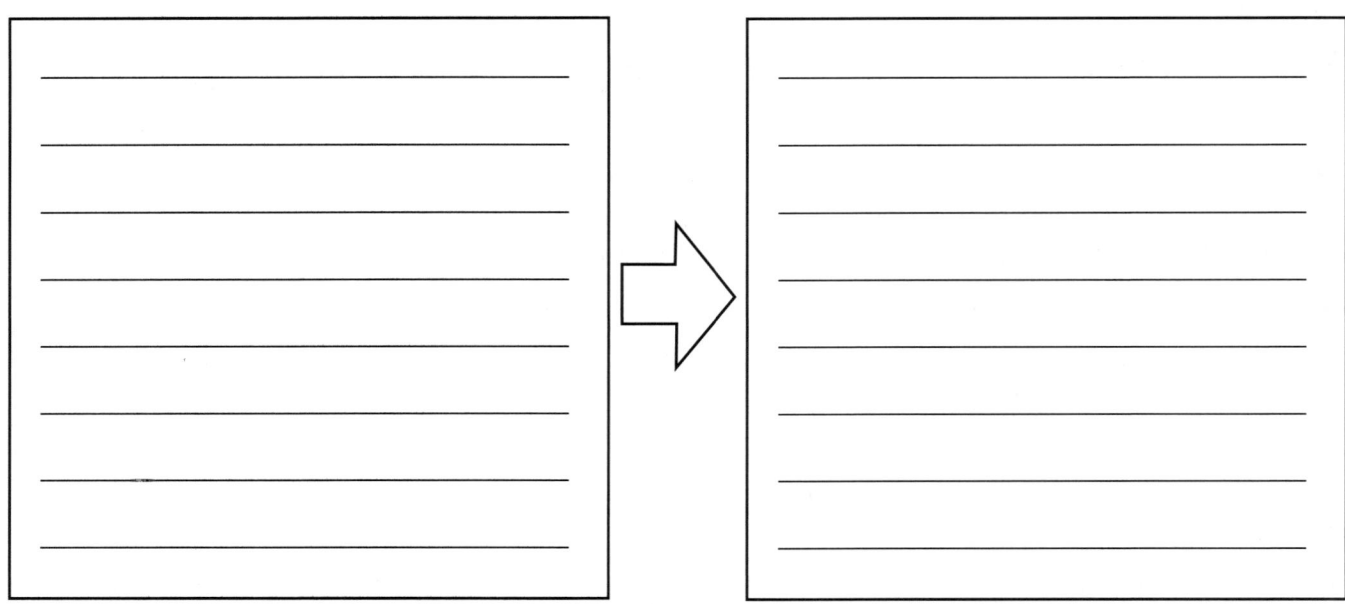

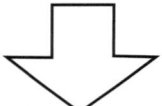

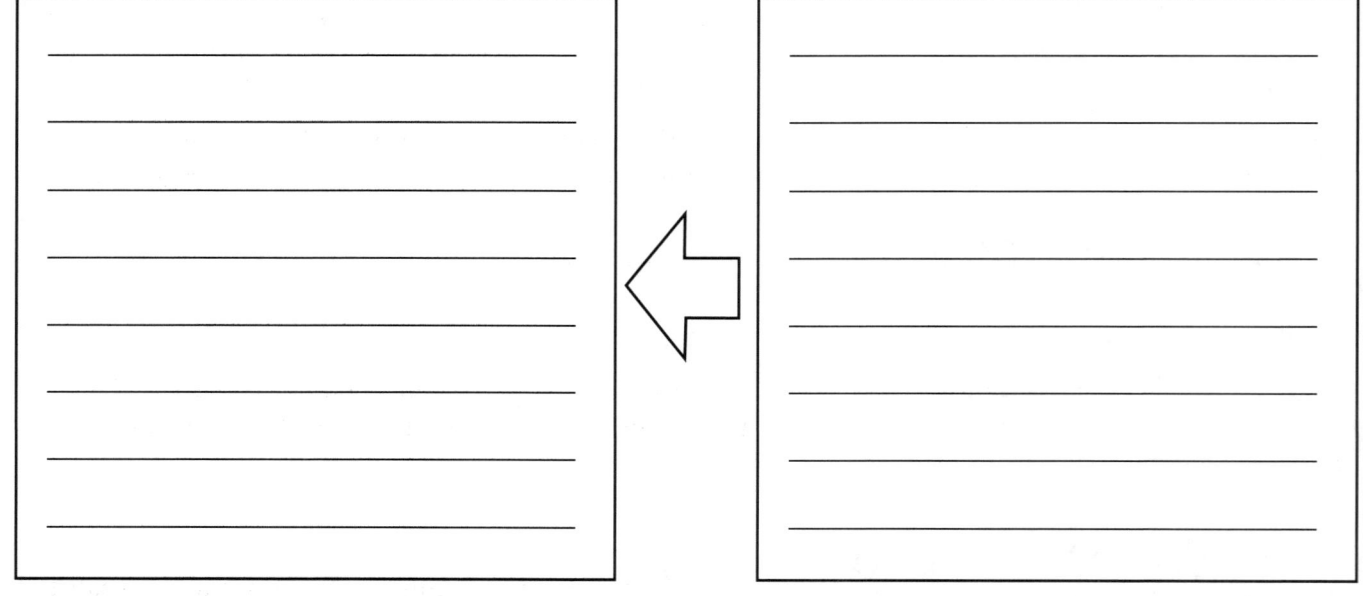

Fluency Trait

Reporting the Weather

Objective

Given a review of the characteristics of the Fluency trait and a graphic organizer, students will write a complete story and share it.

Materials

- white board, overhead projector, or chart paper and marker
- "Weather Story" (page 62), one copy for display
- "It's All About the Weather" (page 63), one copy per student
- weather-related resources from previous lessons
- video camera (optional)

Preparation

Allow time during the lesson for students to write a complete story. Students will also need time to read their stories aloud in a whole class or small group setting. Enlarge "Weather Story" (page 62) for display.

Opening

Ask students to review what they remember about the aspects of the Fluency trait. Ask them how these characteristics make writing effective.

Directions

1. Display "Weather Story" (page 62). Read the story aloud to the class. Ask students if the writing was effective and easy to listen to. Refer to the "Fluency" poster (page 47) and ask students to identify parts of the story that exhibit various characteristics of the trait.

2. Distribute copies of "It's All About the Weather" (page 63). Read through the page with the students, clarifying as needed. Tell students they may use any weather-related resources in the classroom to help them.

3. Have the students complete page 63 and write their stories.

Closing

Divide the students into groups of four or five students each. Have students take turns reading their stories aloud to their classmates. They should ask members of their group for feedback about how effective their story was when read aloud.

Extension

Have students work in groups to create a weather forecast. A forecast might include what the weather will be like tomorrow and the next day or the effect that the weather has on people. Each group should write their predictions and practice reading, with each person in the group reading one part of the forecast. Videotape the students giving their forecasts to the class.

Fluency Trait

Weather Story
by Caleb V.

Sun was very happy. Mean Rain wasn't bothering him. All of a sudden, it was pouring rain. Sun was getting cold. The people were cold. Sun was crying.

"Ha, ha, ha," said Rain.

"Be nice," said Sun.

So they agreed. From then on Sun and Rain took turns making people happy and sad. They were best friends.

Fluency Trait

It's All About the Weather
Story Outline

Characters:
___
___
___

What happens:
___
___
___

The problem:
___
___
___

Who solves the problem:
___
___
___

How the problem is solved:
___
___
___

Voice

As students learn about the trait of Fluency, they begin to learn about writing style. The Voice trait focuses specifically on a writer's individual style. An effective piece of writing that exhibits aspects of the Voice trait will sound like a particular person wrote it. Therefore, writing that has characteristics of Voice will also be fluent; it will have natural rhythm. Authors develop their own unique style by writing from their thoughts and feelings. An author's personality comes through in his or her writing.

Effective writers focus on their audience: they write to the reader. They want to call attention to the writing and draw the reader in. To do this, authors will write honestly, sincerely, and with confidence. As they write based on their own experiences and knowledge of themselves, writers will have the ability to bring a topic to life.

Students will continue to practice expanding their perspectives, as well as read sample pieces written from another person's point of view. They will identify elements of the Voice trait in written samples and begin to develop their own style by writing reflections and personal correspondence.

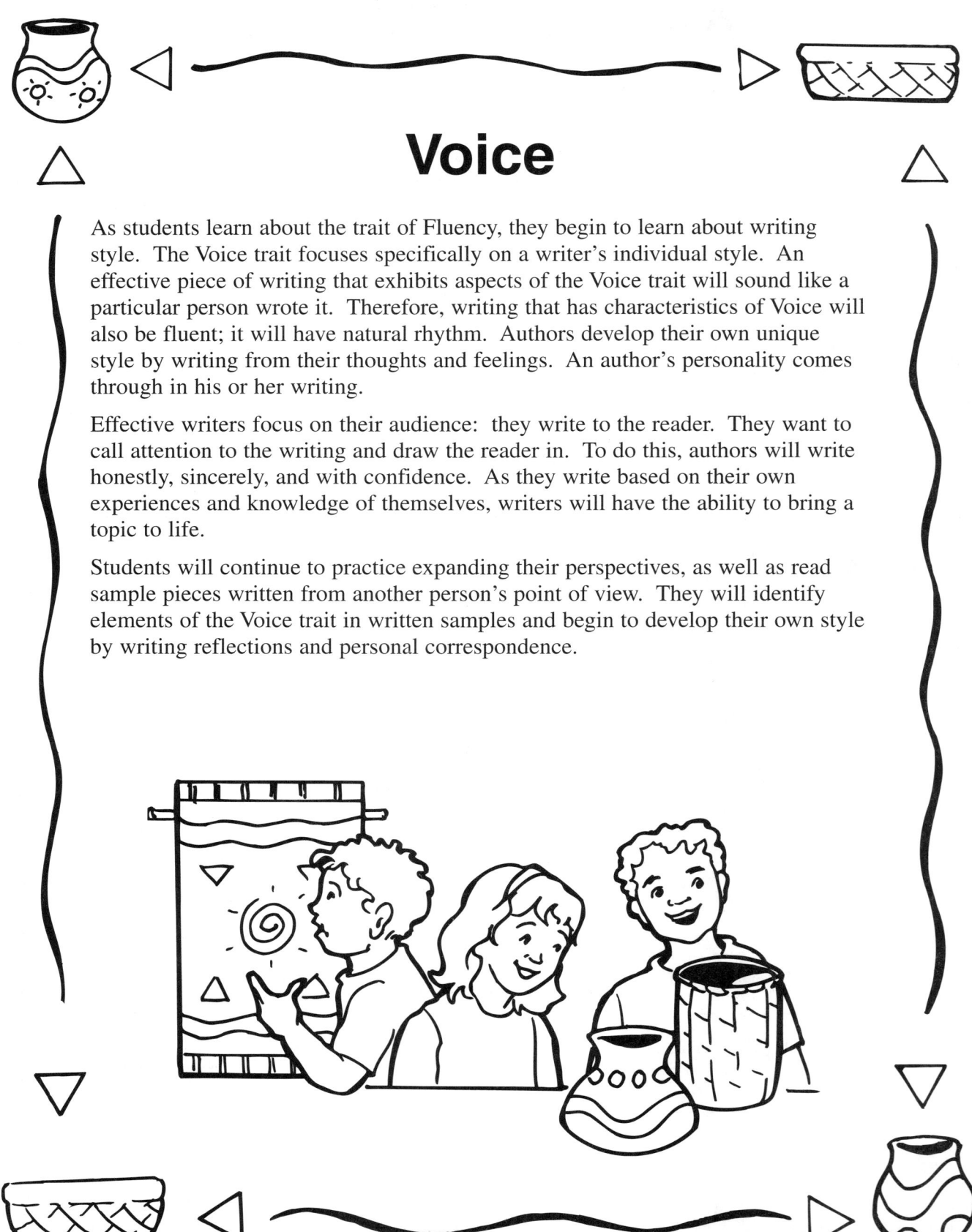

Voice

- sound like a particular person wrote the piece

- allow reader to sense a real person

- author's personality comes through in the writing

- writing comes from author's thoughts and feelings

- natural rhythm

- call attention to the writing

- write sincerely, with confidence

- write to the reader; stay focused on the audience

- convey honesty

- bring the topic to life

- write out of knowing yourself

Voice Trait

Many Views of Chenoa

Objective

Given an introduction to the characteristics of the Voice trait and a listening activity, students will color and add detail to an outline of a person.

Materials

- white board, overhead projector, or chart paper and marker
- "Voice" poster (page 65), one copy for display
- picture books based on authors' lives (e.g., Maurice Sendak, Bill Peet, Tomie de Paola)
- "Autumn Morning" (page 67), one copy per student
- "Chenoa" (page 68), one copy per student
- colored pencils or crayons
- pictures of Native Americans (optional)

Preparation

Enlarge the "Voice" poster (page 65) for display.

Opening

Direct students' attention to the "Voice" poster (page 65). Introduce the trait by asking students to recall stories they have read in which the writer sounds like a real person, or it sounds as if the author is speaking directly to the reader. Show examples of picture books, if available.

Directions

1. Define *voice* as the "ability to speak or sing, the way a person talks, or a means of expressing oneself." Have volunteers each say the same word or word phrase. Ask students how each person sounds different.
2. Tell the class that just as a person's speaking has a unique voice, a person's writing also has its own voice. Not everyone writes in the same way to describe the same thing.
3. Distribute copies of "Chenoa" (page 68). Tell students you will read a paragraph aloud. They should listen to how the author describes herself. Students will add details to the person, based on the paragraph you read.
4. Read aloud "Autumn Morning" (page 67). Then have the students color their pictures of Chenoa (page 68). Ask the class to identify words from the paragraph which helped them draw details and made it seem as if the author wrote about a real person.

Closing

Display student pictures side by side. Ask students to tell how each person portrayed the character differently. Remind students that their drawings show their own "voice."

Extension

Have students look at a picture of a Native American and write a descriptive paragraph about that person. In their writing, students should try to convince the reader this is a real person.

Autumn Morning

My name is Chenoa, which means "dove." Each morning I put on my deerskin dress that is decorated with leather strips sewn onto the bottom. I pull on my soft deerskin boots with colorful beads sewn into each side. I braid my long hair and tie a leather string around it before I leave the hut. The men have gone to fish, and today I will help the women gather berries and nuts. The air has not turned cold yet, so I will not need my cloak. I take only a basket with me.

Voice Trait

Chenoa

#3584 Traits of Good Writing: Grades 1–2 · 68 · ©Teacher Created Resources, Inc.

Voice Trait

Listening to Native Voices

Objective

Given an experience listening to music, each student will practice calling attention to his or her writing by selecting appropriate words, focusing on characteristics of the Voice trait.

Materials

- white board, overhead projector, or chart paper and markers
- CD of Native American music from the library (e.g., "Beneath the Raven Moon" by Mary Youngblood or see *http://www.matoska.com*).
- CD player
- "I Hear You" (page 71), one copy for display and one copy per student
- Reflective Paragraph (page 70) (optional)

Preparation

Enlarge "I Hear You" (page 71) for display.

Opening

Review with students the concept of Voice: people speak and make musical sounds in many different ways, and other things, such as musical instruments and writing, have voice. Ask students what is meant by rhythm; have them tap out a rhythm on their laps. Define *rhythm* as a "regular beat in music or poetry" or a "flow of rising and falling sounds."

Directions

1. Introduce a new aspect of the Voice trait by discussing the concept of calling attention to the writing. Ask students what they think is meant by "call attention to." Explain that effective writing uses words, enabling the reader to concentrate, have awareness of, and give careful thought to what has been written.

2. Tell the class they will listen to a recording of Native American instrumental music. They will listen for rhythm in the music.

3. Distribute copies of "I Hear You" (page 71). Tell students they will write in the speech balloons ways in which the music catches their attention. Model this for the students by showing them the display copy of the page. Mention a well-known folk song, something your whole class can hum together, and ask students to identify what about the song makes them want to listen and sing (e.g., catchy tune, simple words, funny song, hand motions).

4. Play an instrumental music CD. Remind students to write words about the music in the speech balloons on page 71.

They may also write words to tell what they think or how they feel about the music in the appropriate areas on the page.

Voice Trait

Listening to Native Voices (cont.)

Closing

Have students share their reflections after listening to the music.

Extension

Read aloud the Reflective Paragraph below. Explain that a *reflective paragraph* is one in which the author "writes his or her thoughts and feelings about something in particular." Ask students to use the notes they wrote to write a reflective paragraph about their thoughts and feelings about the music they listened to. Have students illustrate their paragraphs. Student work may be collected in a class book as part of a study on Native Americans.

Reflective Paragraph

This music sounds peaceful and quiet. It makes me think of my friends and family. The song talks about people helping each other. The only instrument I hear is a piano. I wish it also had a flute.

Voice Trait

I Hear You

The music makes me think . . .

_____

_____

The music makes me feel . . .

_____

_____

_____

Voice Trait

Writing Across Time

Objective

Given instruction in letter format and a sample letter to read, students will write a letter expressing specific characteristics of the Voice trait.

Materials

- sample letters (e.g., some you have received)
- "Friendly Letter Poster" (page 74), one copy for display
- Sample Letter (page 75), one copy per student
- "Dear Friend" (page 76), one copy per student
- stationery, markers, pens, highlighters, stickers (optional)

Preparation

Collect some sample letters to display the friendly letter format. If you do not have any available, you might want to create some sample letters. Or use a picture book of letters, such as *The Jolly Postman* (Janet and Allen Ahlberg). Enlarge the "Friendly Letter Poster" (page 74) for display.

Opening

Show students the sample letters or book. Ask students if they like to receive mail and why. Discuss the fact that the most enjoyable letters to read are those written by a friend—someone we know and trust. Friends are often people who are honest, truthful, and confident; they believe in themselves and others. Have students tell about letters they have received from this type of friend.

Directions

1. Examine the sample letters with the students. Point out various aspects of the friendly letter format: heading, greeting, body, closing, and signature. You might want to highlight each part of the letter in a different color or with a colored tag or arrow. Ask students why a letter might need all these parts.

2. Tell the class that the characteristics just discussed regarding friends are also some of the qualities found in the Voice trait. Authors who write effectively with voice write honestly, truthfully, and with certainty; and with belief in themselves and their readers. Writers who write with voice don't try to pretend to be something they're not.

3. Read aloud the Sample Letter (page 75). Conduct a class discussion about how the person showed sincerity and confidence in his or her writing.

4. Distribute copies of the Sample Letter (page 75) and "Dear Friend" (page 76). Have students read the Sample Letter again and complete the sentences on the top portion of the page.

Writing Across Time (cont.)

Closing

Review the concepts of writing sincerely and with confidence. Have students write a letter back to the author, asking questions about his or her life. Students should incorporate these characteristics of the Voice trait in their writing and use the friendly letter format. (Students may refer to the Friendly Letter poster [page 74], if necessary.)

Extension

Tell students to pretend to be the person who wrote the letter they read and responded to. Have them write a diary page about one day in that person's life. Even though they are pretending to be that person, students should write confidently and sincerely as they write from that person's perspective.

Voice Trait

Friendly Letter

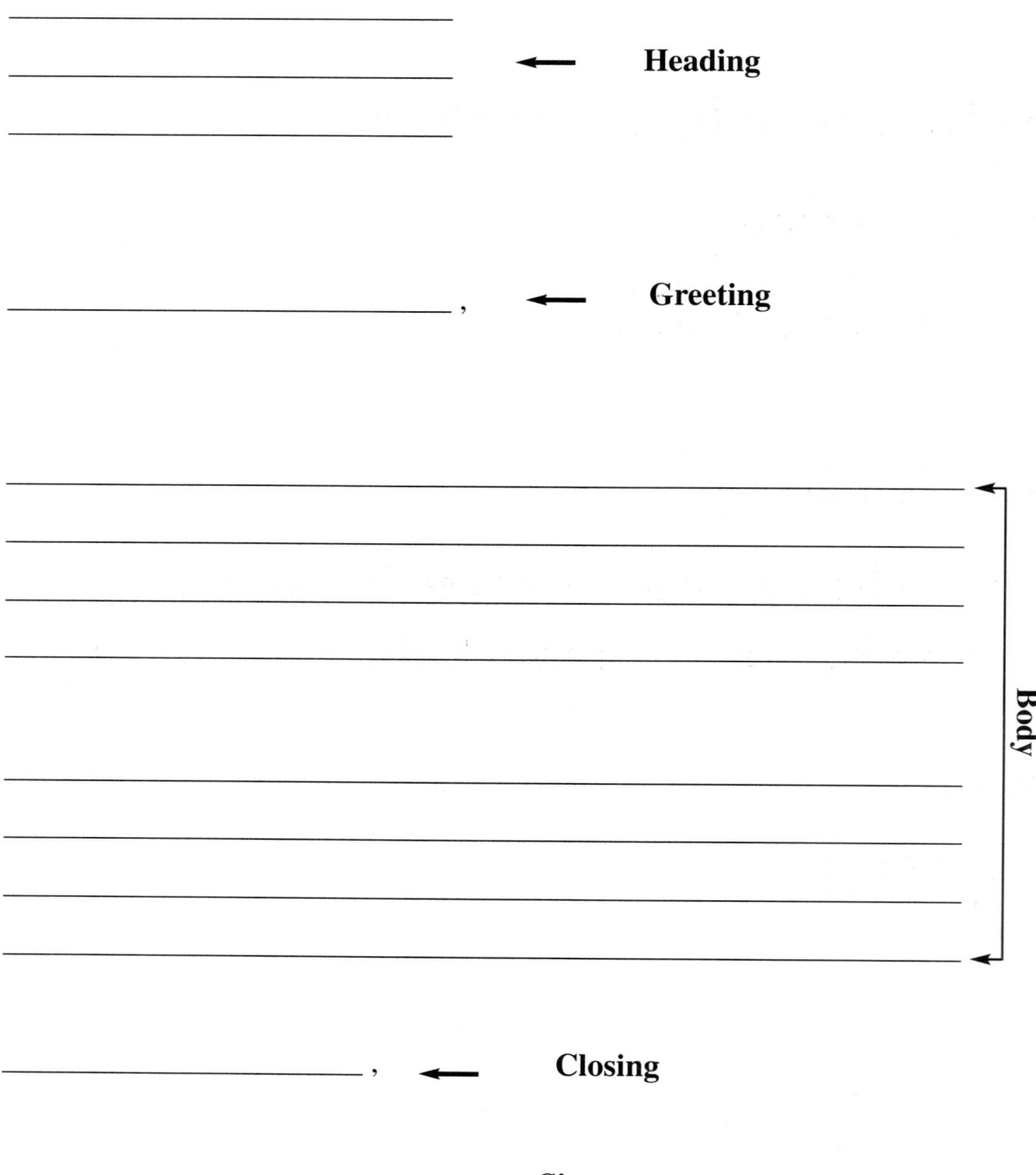

Sample Letter

by Julian A.

Tall Mountains by Great River

Beaver Territory

October 16, 2005

Dear Ahmik,

I like it when we hunt because it is a challenge. I like to sit by the fire and tell stories. I like my life.

From,

Gray Wolf

Voice Trait

Dear Friend

When I read _____'s letter,

I learned _____

I found out that

_____

_____

I also learned _____

_____

_____

I would like to ask _____ some questions. I want to ask

_____

_____?

Voice Trait

Windows on Their World

Objective

Given a sample description and classroom resources, students will create a diorama and note cards to depict a scene from a historical person's life.

Materials

- sample note cards (page 78)
- resources on Native Americans
- student writing from previous lessons, if applicable
- shoeboxes
- index cards, construction paper, craft sticks, glue, tape, and other craft materials to make diorama scenes
- sample diorama scene, if available (optional)
- "Come Visit Us" (page 79), one copy per student (optional)

Preparation

Make sample note cards using index cards (see page 78).

Opening

Draw students' attention to the "Voice" poster (page 65). Ask the students how writing can bring a topic to life. Discuss how the words an author uses can make the writing come alive. Writers focus on their audience when they remember who might be most likely to read their writing then pretend they are writing to that audience. For example, if someone the student's own age reads the writing, he or she would write as if talking with that person. If an adult, such as a teacher or grandparent, reads the writing, the student would try his or her best to use proper spelling, punctuation, grammar, and might try to use more "grown-up" words, rather than writing the way he or she might talk with friends on the playground.

Directions

1. Tell students a *diorama* is a "picture scene in miniature showing human or animal figures in a natural setting." If available, show students a sample diorama.

2. Read the sample note cards. Ask students to describe the diorama scene about which they think the author is writing. If you wish, draw on the board as the students describe the scene. Have students offer words that helped them form a mental picture of the scene or that brought the topic to life in their minds.

3. Tell students they will use classroom resources and writing they have completed in previous lessons to create a diorama scene. They should select their characters and scene before beginning to work.

©Teacher Created Resources, Inc.

Voice Trait

Windows on Their World *(cont.)*

Directions *(cont.)*

4. Tell the class their audience will be other students, as well as adults, and they should write their note cards with this audience in mind. That is, they should write as if adults will also read their writing, not just their classmates; their writing will need to be complete, not assuming the audience knows everything the student knows about the resources.

5. Have students use craft materials to create a diorama scene. You may wish to have students work with a partner or small group to create the diorama. After they have completed their scene, students should write note cards to describe their scene.

Closing

Display student diorama scenes and note cards around the room. Have the students evaluate one another, based on bringing the topic to life and focusing on the audience.

Extension

Distribute copies of "Come Visit Us" (page 79). Explain that students will use this form to make an invitation for family members, inviting them to visit the classroom. Visitors will view the diorama scenes and other classroom displays created during the students' study of the Voice trait.

Sample Note Cards

Sahale and Kimama paddle a canoe down the river.

They will stop to catch fish with their nets.

Voice Trait

Come Visit Us

Cut on the solid line. Fold on the dotted lines. Draw a colorful picture on the front of the invitation. On the inside, complete the information as your teacher directs you.

©*Teacher Created Resources, Inc.* 79 #3584 *Traits of Good Writing: Grades 1–2*

Voice Trait

Learning about Each Other

Objective

Given a paragraph written from a specific person's perspective, the students will use color to highlight what they learn about the writer, based on the characteristics of the Voice trait.

Materials

- PowerPoint presentation or poster presentation
- "A Day in the Life of a Native American" (page 82), one copy per pair of students
- "A Page from My Life" (page 83), one copy per student (optional)
- highlighters (six different colors per pair)
- construction paper (optional)

Preparation

Prepare a brief PowerPoint or poster presentation of your life, with slides for topics such as My Favorites, How I Feel about My Family, Things I Like to Do, How I Feel about My Name, Birthday or other Holiday Celebrations, etc.

Opening

Direct students' attention to the "Voice" poster (page 65) and review the characteristics. Show students the PowerPoint or Poster presentation you have prepared. Ask students to identify words and phrases you used that exhibit qualities of the Voice trait.

Directions

1. Focus on the last two aspects of the trait. Explain that in order for writers to write honestly, sincerely, and with confidence, they need to know themselves. That means writers need to know topics about which they can write, their strengths and weaknesses, and how to relate to other people. This knowledge helps authors write more truthfully about the world around them.

2. Tell students they will read a paragraph with a partner and then highlight words and phrases the author uses that show qualities of the Voice trait. Identify the characteristics as taught in each lesson and suggest a color for each: green for the first two characteristics, blue for the second two, yellow for the next two, purple for the next two, red for "bring the topic to life," and orange for "write out of knowing yourself." (See possible responses on page 81.) You might want to place a large colored dot next to the corresponding characteristic on the "Voice Poster" (page 65).

3. Pair students with partners. Distribute copies of "A Day in the Life of a Native American" (page 82). Have students read and highlight as directed. Model one or two phrases if necessary.

Voice Trait

Learning about Each Other *(cont.)*

Closing

Have students give words and phrases they identified and tell which aspects of the Voice trait the writing shows.

Extension

Distribute copies of "A Page from My Life" (page 83). Have students complete the page. Encourage students to write other pages to create an autobiography, which can then be stapled between construction-paper covers. Topics can be similar to those you addressed in your presentation during the opening of the lesson.

Possible Student Activity Responses

(page 80, #2)

green highlighting: I would go play in the forest. (allows reader to sense a real person)

blue highlighting: It would be hard work getting food and clean water. (author's personality comes through in writing)

purple highlighting: I would be scared of the big ships and seeing a stranger. (convey honesty)

red highlighting: I would play on trees and climb trees. (brings the topic to life)

A Day in the Life of a Native American

by Caleb V.

I would go play in the forest. I would play on trees and climb trees. It would be hard work getting food and clean water. I would be scared of the big ships and seeing a stranger.

Voice Trait

A Page from My Life

I am good at . . .

_____
_____

I need help when . . .

_____
_____

My family thinks I am . . .

_____
_____

My friends like it when I . . .

_____
_____

I like to play . . .

_____
_____

I know a lot about . . .

_____
_____

Write two or three sentences about a topic you know about:

_____
_____
_____

Organization

As students learn to incorporate the Organization trait in their writing, they begin to view the whole picture. Effective writing has a logical order and sequence with clear direction and purpose; it does not confuse the reader. Rather, writing that displays qualities of organization guides the reader through the writing, leading to the main point. Writers who incorporate the characteristics of the Organization trait include an introduction that captures the reader's attention and conclude the piece by making the reader think. Organized writing flows smoothly, with transitions that tie together.

Students will practice the characteristics of this trait by learning about beginnings and endings of stories and paragraph structure. They will practice writing their own paragraphs. The teacher will introduce story elements to the students and give them opportunities to outline a story, identify story elements, and write a complete story. As students write their own stories, they will focus on including appropriate pacing and transitions in their writing.

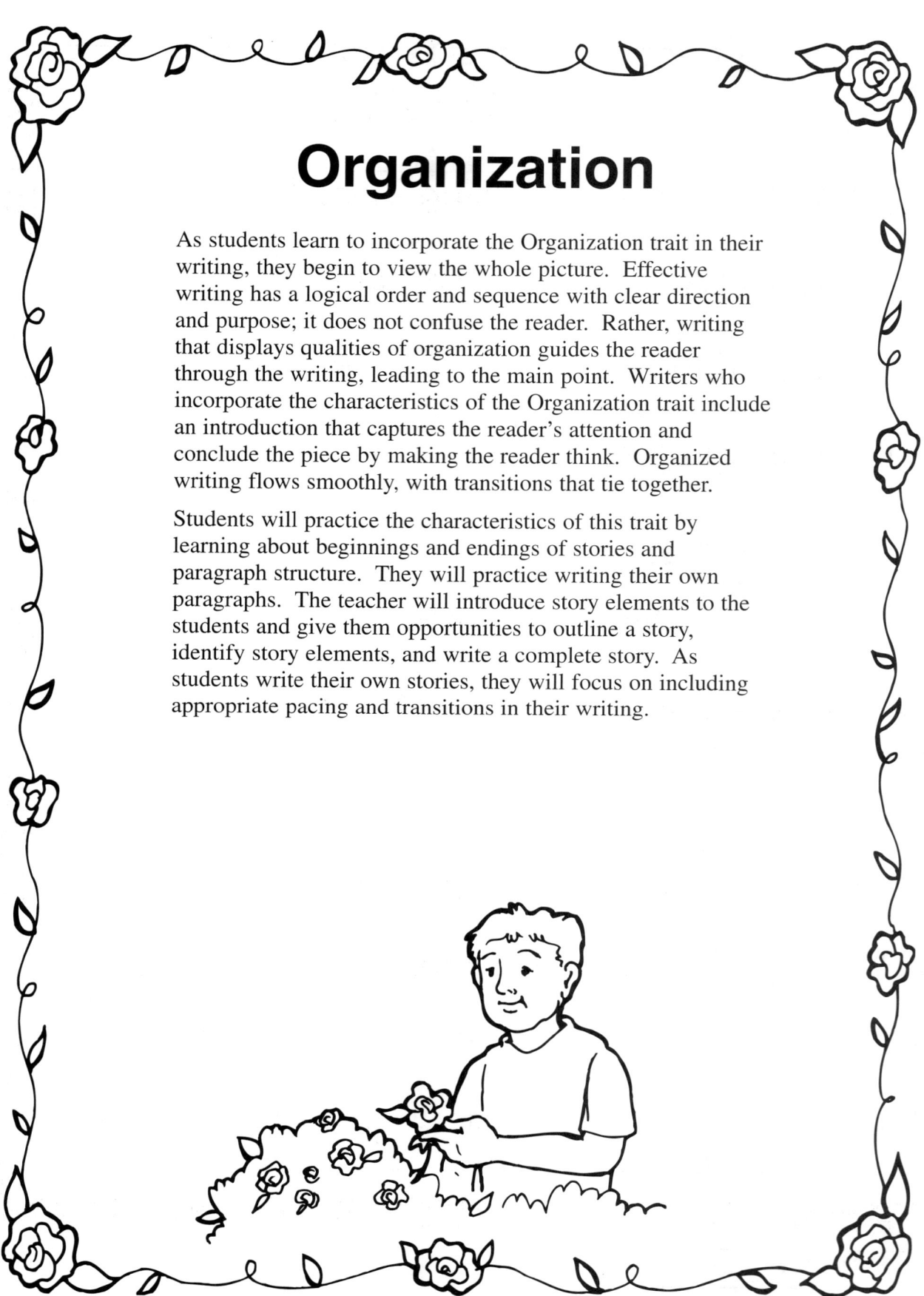

Organization

- has attention-getting introduction
- conclusion makes the reader think
- logical order and sequence
- appropriate pacing
- flows smoothly
- transitions tie together
- path leads reader to the main point
- guides reader through the writing
- clear direction and purpose
- links back to main idea

Organization Trait

From Seeds to Flowers

Objective

Given an introduction to the Organization trait and instruction on creating a diagram, students will label a diagram.

Materials

- white board, overhead projector, or chart paper and marker
- "Organization" poster (page 85), one copy for display
- picture books and stories about plants and flowers
- "Flower Diagram" (page 87), one copy for display
- "A Flower Arrangement" (page 88), one copy per student

Preparation

Enlarge the "Organization" poster (page 85) and "Flower Diagram" (page 87) for display.

Opening

Share with students the "Organization" poster (page 85). Explain that during their study of this trait, students will learn how a story or piece of writing fits together as a whole.

Directions

1. Read the books aloud. Have students identify the beginnings and endings of the stories. Review that an author will use words or phrases that make readers aware and help them concentrate and focus on what the author has to say. Explain how effective writing has a satisfying conclusion where the reader feels the story has ended satisfactorily, yet it allows for the possibility that the story could continue. As a class, examine the order and sequence in the stories.

2. Show students the "Flower Diagram" (page 87). Explain that a *diagram* is a picture with labels to explain the parts of an object. Have students review the life cycle of a flower. As students identify the beginning of a flower's life, indicate the appropriate place on the diagram. Continue on through the various stages of the life cycle of a flower. Point out how the student wrote a creative beginning and ending.

3. Distribute copies of "A Flower Arrangement" (page 88). Have students label the diagram. Encourage students to write words, phrases, or sentences next to the diagram that could be used as beginnings and endings for a story about flowers.

Closing

Display the students' diagrams in the classroom. Have students evaluate two or three classmates' diagrams, beginnings, and endings for effectiveness.

Extension

Have students use their diagram and words to write a complete paragraph about the life cycle of a flower.

Organization Trait

Flower Diagram

flower

One day it grows.

stem

leaf

You give it water and plenty of sunshine.

You plant the seed.

Madison G.

roots

Organization Trait

A Flower Arrangement

1.

2.

3.

4.

Organization Trait

A Plant's Life

Objective

Given instruction in the use of transitional words, students will identify transitional words in a sample piece and draw a picture.

Materials

- white board, overhead projector, or chart paper and markers
- "A Fruit Tree" (page 90), one copy per student
- highlighter pens or crayons
- "A Most Unusual Plant" (page 91), one copy per student (optional)

Opening

Have students review the life cycle of a plant. As they tell you the steps, write them on the white board. Use a different colored marker to underline any transition words. Ask students if they know why you marked those particular words.

Directions

1. Explain that the highlighted words in the opening activity are called transition words. *Transition* means "changing from one subject to another." These are words that writers use to move from one paragraph, or section of writing, to the next. Transition words help tie ideas together so that the writing flows smoothly. Ask students if the plant life cycle needs any other transition words to make the writing flow more smoothly or to link the steps together.

2. Ask students to give other transition words, in addition to those already highlighted. Make a class list using words discussed and with words from the list on page 90.

3. Distribute copies of "A Fruit Tree" (page 90) and highlighter pens or crayons. (If students use crayons, tell them they will need to color lightly over the writing so you know which words they have highlighted.) Tell the class they should follow along and highlight any transition words in the paragraph as you read the sample aloud to them.

Closing

Review with students which words in the sample paragraph should be highlighted. Have students draw a picture to go with the sample paragraph.

Extension

Distribute copies of "A Most Unusual Plant" (page 91). Have students complete the sentences to write a story about a green plant. If time permits, have students use their sentences from the page to write a final copy of their story to share with the class.

Organization Trait

Transition Words

first	finally	next	because
then	last	when	soon
however	but	while	also

A Fruit Tree

by McKenna C.

One year there was a famine. I was unusually unhappy. I was starved. So I went on a walk to see if there were any berries. But I found no berries. I found a seed pack. Then I put one seed into the ground. When I woke up in the morning, I saw a tree. It had an orange on it. I said I wish it had apples, and the tree burst out with apples. Then I said grapes, watermelon, pineapple, and cantaloupe. All of them came bursting out on the tree. Finally, we sold all the fruit and got so much money we built a store.

A Most Unusual Plant

One day _____went to take care of her green plant.

First, she _____

_____.

Then she _____

because it _____.

While she was _____ the plant began to

_____.

Finally, she had to _____ before

_____.

Organization Trait

Let's Grow Some Variety

Objective

Given instruction in sentence structure, students will write a variety of sentences about plants and flowers.

Materials

- overhead projector, chart paper, or other form of projection and markers
- "My Garden" (page 93), one copy for display
- "A Garden of Diversity" (page 94), one copy per student
- crayons or colored pencils
- magazine pictures (optional)
- construction paper, 9" x 12" (23 cm x 30 cm), scissors, glue

Preparation

Enlarge "My Garden Sample B" (page 93) for display.

Opening

Read "My Garden, Sample A" (page 93) aloud to the class. Ask students if the writing is interesting or effective. Why or why not? Tell the class that sentences do not all have to be the same.

Directions

1. Share with students "My Garden, Sample B" (page 93). Ask students to identify ways in which the sentences differ from one another.

2. Explain that sentences may take a variety of forms. Demonstrate by using different colored markers to show types of words used, placement within the sentence, sentence length, etc.

3. Distribute copies of "A Garden of Diversity" (page 94). Tell students that *diversity* means "different" or "a variety." Ask students to color the pictures. Have them write a different sentence to describe each picture. Encourage students to write neatly.

Closing

Post student pictures and sentences as a bulletin-board display titled, "A Garden of Diversity." If you choose to have students do the extension activity, allow room in the display for those student projects as well.

Extension

Provide magazine pictures for student use. Have the students create a collage to depict a garden. Students should then write a short paragraph to describe their garden using a variety of sentences.

My Garden

Sample A

Justin V.

My garden will have lots of flowers. I want it to be protected. I will water it. I will also make a fence. I will gather supplies so I can check it. I will make a book of my garden.

Sample B

Chloe O.

My garden has statues and bird fountains.

There are two paths and a flower bed.

My garden is pretty.

It has lots of different flowers of different colors.

There are tall and small flowers.

There are rocks surrounding the flower bed.

The flowers are petunias.

Organization Trait

A Garden of Diversity

_____
_____

_____
_____

_____
_____

_____
_____

Organization Trait

Plant Before You Harvest

Objective

Given sentences from a sample paragraph, students will arrange the sentences in the proper sequence.

Materials

- white board, overhead projector, or chart paper and marker
- picture cards showing a sequence of events (e.g., from magazines, photos of a class or school event)
- arrow patterns (page 96)
- cardstock
- "Planting My Garden" (page 97), one copy for display
- "Finding Your Way Through" (page 98), one copy per student
- paper, scissors, glue

Preparation

Gather pictures from magazines or photographs showing stages in a sequence of events (e.g., a birthday party, field trip, trip to the store). Prepare the picture cards by attaching cutouts or photos to cardstock for durability. Enlarge and photocopy the arrows (page 96) onto cardstock, if necessary, to match the size of the picture cards. Photocopy "Planting My Garden" (page 97) onto an overhead transparency.

Opening

Show the class the picture cards. Ask student volunteers to help you arrange the pictures in the proper sequence. Discuss with students how they knew in which order to put the pictures (i.e., picture clues, this happens then that happens).

Directions

1. Direct students' attention to the "Organization" poster (page 85). Review briefly the aspects of the trait studied thus far.

2. Continue a class discussion about logical order and sequence. Tell students that events in a story need to happen in a logical order for the writing to make sense. That is, one idea will follow another in a way that the reader would expect.

3. Tell the class that writing that exhibits qualities of organization guides the reader through the writing: there is a path to lead the reader to the main point, the writing makes sense, and the writing is not confusing. Explain that to *guide* is "to show the way, to help lead someone through something difficult." As you talk, place arrows between the picture cards to form a path.

Organization Trait

Plant Before You Harvest (cont.)

Directions (cont.)

4. Show students "Planting My Garden" (page 97). Have students read one box at a time, discussing with the class the sequence of the sentences. Ask students how the author created a path to guide the reader through the writing.

5. Tell students they will now guide a reader (the teacher) through a piece of writing by arranging sentences in the proper order. Distribute copies of "Finding Your Way Through" (page 98). Have students read each sentence box and number it to show where in the paragraph it should go. You might want to model the first one and work together as a class. After students have placed a number in each sentence box, they should cut them out and glue them to a separate sheet of paper. Have students draw arrows between boxes to show the sequence of the sentences.

Closing

Ask students to tell the order in which they placed the sentences. Review with students to check for understanding of sequence and a path that leads or guides the reader through the writing.

Extension

Have students draw pictures (or use magazine cutouts) to create their own Sequence Game Cards. On the back of each card, a student writes a sentence. Have the student then trade cards with a partner and arrange his or her partner's cards in the correct sequence.

Arrows

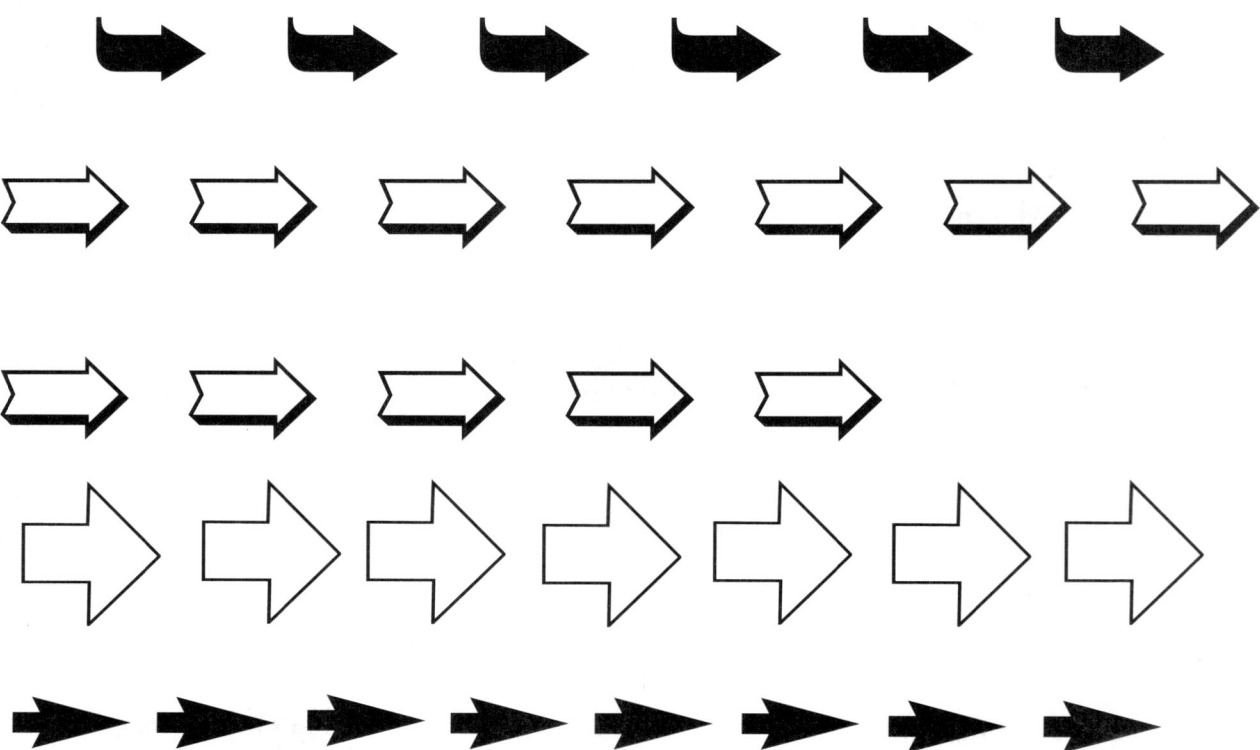

Planting My Garden
by Caleb V.

If I had a garden, I would plant peas, corn, carrots, and small tomatoes.

I would plant these things because I like to eat them.

I would take care of my garden by watering it and giving it food.

My garden would probably be inside because I would forget to water it.

I would make my garden a summer garden.

Organization Trait

Finding Your Way Through

by Bob P.

☐ They need water and sunlight to grow.

☐ Seeds from the flower drop in the ground, and a new flower grows.

☐ Plants start from seeds.

☐ After they bloom, flowers die and fall off.

☐ Then flowers bud and bloom.

Organization Trait

Planting a Story

Objective

Given an introduction to basic story elements, purpose, and direction, students will match pictures to story elements and write a complete story.

Materials

- white board or poster board and markers
- "Story Elements Chart" (page 101), one copy for display
- "The Seed" (page 102)
- magazine pictures, scissors, glue
- "Putting It All Together" (page 103), one copy per student
- flower patterns (page 102), cardstock, construction paper, markers, pipe cleaners or hangers and string (optional)

Preparation

Enlarge the "Story Elements Chart" (page 101) for display. If students will be completing the Extension activity, enlarge the flower patterns (page 102), photocopy onto cardstock, and cut them out. To save time, you might wish to prepare magazine pictures by cutting out several that would be appropriate. (Students may trim the pictures if necessary.)

Opening

Direct the students' attention to the "Organization" poster (page 85). Review sequence, pacing, transitions, and what makes effective introductions and conclusions.

Directions

1. Display the "Story Elements Chart" (page 101). Define *characters, setting*, and *plot*. Check for understanding of any other elements. Read aloud "The Seed" (page 102). After you read, have students help you complete the chart, based on the story.

2. Focus the students' attention on the final two aspects of the Organization trait, "clear direction and purpose," and "links back to the main idea." Ask students what they think is meant by direction and purpose. Explain that the direction in a story is that "path along which the writer guides the reader." Authors usually have one main idea in a story: a reason or purpose why they wrote the story.

3. Refer back to "The Seed" (page 102). Ask students why they think the author wrote the story. What goal did he or she hope to achieve? To what audience did the writer direct the story? How did the writer guide the reader through the story?

Organization Trait

Planting a Story (cont.)

Directions (cont.)

4. Distribute copies of "Putting It All Together" (page 103). Tell students they will find magazine pictures to go with each of the story elements (i.e., for Character, picture of a flower for a story about a flower; for Setting, picture of the Moon for a story that takes place at night). Then the students should write a phrase for each element on page 103.

Closing

Have students use their pictures to write a complete story using each of the story elements. Before students begin to write, encourage them to set a purpose and audience for writing this particular story. Perhaps they know someone who likes to garden who would enjoy the story, or maybe a friend is sick and would like a cheerful story.

Extension

Students can make a mobile depicting story elements. Distribute a construction-paper flower (see Preparation) to each student. The student writes one of the story elements on each petal, leaf, and center of the flower. Have each student assemble the mobile using pipe cleaners or hangers and string.

Organization Trait

Story Elements Chart

Beginning	Purpose	Characters	Setting (Time)

Setting (Place)	Main Idea	Problem or Conflict	Solution

Organization Trait

The Seed

by Chloe O.

One day there was a little boy who was planting some flowers. He opened a pack and he saw a different seed. He planted it and it took a long time to grow. When it grew it looked green, then yellow, then orange.

He showed it to his mom and it was a . . . pumpkin.

So after that he went to the store and saw a pack of pumpkin seeds. He bought those and some more seeds. When fall came, he carved the pumpkin. One night the boy put the pumpkin on his porch.

Flower Patterns

Organization Trait

Putting It All Together

| Beginning: | Characters |

| Purpose: Why am I writing this story? | Setting of Time (When) |

| Setting of Place (Where) | Main Idea |

| Problem or Conflict | Solution |

Conventions

Students put the pieces together as they worked through the Organization trait and began to consider the whole picture. They also had opportunities to consider self-evaluation, based on established criteria. The next major step in the writing process is editing. The Conventions trait breaks the huge task of editing into smaller parts—allowing students to practice editing their own and others' work, focusing on one factor at a time.

Students learn about and practice correct forms of conventions such as correctly spelling plural and singular forms of nouns, capitalization of place names, punctuation, possessives, and subject-verb agreement. Although students practice characteristics of the Conventions trait mostly by reading and editing samples written by others, they will also continue to work toward editing their own work.

Conventions

- check for correct spelling

- use correct capitalization

- include proper punctuation

- check for grammar and correct word usage

- use action verbs

- check for appropriate paragraphs

- include an appropriate title

- use proofreading marks

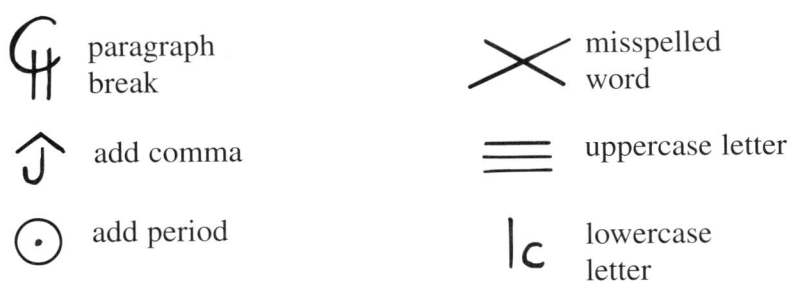

Conventions Trait

The Importance of a Name

Objective
Given instruction in the proper use of capitals, students will edit a sample paragraph, checking for correct capitalization.

Materials
- white board, overhead projector, or chart paper and marker
- "Conventions" poster (page 105), one copy for display
- photograph or magazine picture of a family
- "My Family" (page 108), one copy per student
- crayons or colored pencils
- "All Around the Town" (page 109), one copy per student

Preparation
Enlarge the "Conventions" poster (page 105) for display.

Opening
Show the class the photograph or magazine picture. Ask students to identify the subject (a family). Ask them if all families are the same. Tear the photograph in half. Ask if the family is still in one piece. How could the picture be fixed? Tell students that they will learn about the Conventions trait. Explain that *conventions* refer to the "mechanics of writing," or "how to fix writing to make it better."

Directions
1. Show students the "Conventions" poster (page 105). Tell the class they will study just one or two aspects at a time. Editing, or fixing, writing is a big job and they will learn about it one step at a time.

2. Review with students any words for which they will need to use a capital letter, such as names of people and places, streets, cities, and states.

3. Tell students they will edit a sample paragraph about a family. They will color each letter that should be capitalized and write the correct capital letter above it.

4. Distribute copies of "My Family" (page 108). Monitor and assist students as necessary as they work.

5. Distribute copies of "All Around the Town" (page 109). Have students color the features of the town. Below each picture they should write the name of a person and specific place or street in their town they have visited with someone in their family.

The Importance of a Name (cont.)

Closing

Have students share the place names and streets they go to with their families using page 109.

Extension

Divide students into teams of at least five to play a game. Each team needs a sheet of paper and a pencil. Explain that they will play a version of the Alphabet Game on paper. The first person writes "I am going to _____ " (a place name beginning with **A**). That person passes the paper to the next person. The second person writes "I am going to **A** and **B**" (a place name beginning with **B**). Tell students they don't need to worry about spelling at this point; place names can be difficult to spell. You may also wish to assist students with spelling or have a master list of place names posted in the room.

My Family

My family includes doug, tracie, brian, and me. dad works on computers. mom goes to cascade college. My family likes to play games and cook. grandma and grandpa and I like to cook, read, and go shopping at bird in hand. I have a pet named nala. She likes kids, bones, and her master. I go to hearthwood school.

kenneth m.

Conventions Trait

All Around the Town

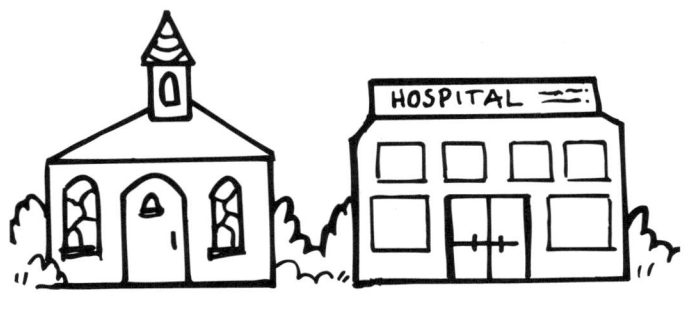

_____

_____

_____

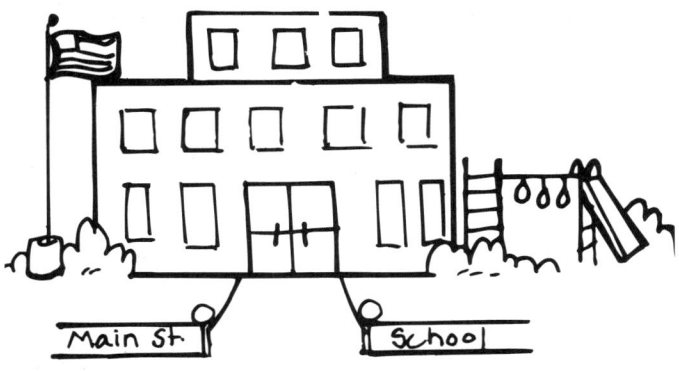

_____

_____

Conventions Trait

All Kinds of People

Objective

Given a review of the three basic types of sentences, students will identify and write examples of each type.

Materials

- "Our Family" (page 111)
- index cards
- "Coloring Sentences" (page 112), one copy per student (optional)
- crayons or colored pencils, scissors, glue (optional)

Preparation

Write a period, a question mark, and an exclamation point on one each of three index cards to create punctuation cards.

Opening

Read "Our Family" (page 111) aloud and expressively to the class, using punctuation. Ask students what types of sentences they heard you read (e.g., telling sentences, asking sentences, exciting sentences). Review with students these three types of sentences, explaining to students that they are called statements, questions, and exclamations.

Directions

1. Refer to the three types of sentences just discussed. Ask students which mark you would use at the end of each type of sentence (e.g., period, question mark, exclamation point).

2. Show the class the punctuation cards. Have students write one or two sentences of each type about their family.

3. Divide students into small groups of four to six. Students will combine their sentences to create a silly story about a family. They may give their family a fictitious name.

Closing

Have students illustrate their funny family stories. These may be bound into a class book for the classroom library.

Extension

Distribute copies of "Coloring Sentences" (page 112). Have students color the punctuation cards at the bottom of the page. They should lightly color the periods blue, the question marks green, and the exclamation points red. After they color, have the students cut out the cards. They will glue each card next to the corresponding sentence.

Our Family

by Faith U.

Sometimes my brother eats dead bugs and baby spiders! My dad eats live and dead bugs, too. My mom's name is Darla, my dad's name is Tony, and my brother's name is Trey. Did you know we have two lizards? We also have a dog. The dog's name is Dumas and the lizards' names are Sunny and Delanno.

Conventions Trait

Coloring Sentences

1. Where should my sister keep her pet fish ☐

2. My family has a really big house ☐

3. There are four people in my family ☐

4. Wow, my family gets to go to Disneyland ☐

5. I like to go to the beach with my family ☐

6. Did you know my parents live in California ☐

| ! | ! | ? | ? | . | . |

Conventions Trait

One Letter at a Time

Objective

Given a review of common spelling words, students will correctly edit a writing sample for spelling errors.

Materials

- lowercase letters, approximately 4" (10 cm) in size
- 100 high frequency words (page 115), one copy per student
- cardstock
- "Washing the Car" (page 114), one copy per student
- "Mr. Spelling B's House" (page 114) (optional)

Preparation

Photocopy the high frequency word list (page 115) onto cardstock and laminate if desired. Cut out the lists to make bookmarks.

Opening

Show students an uppercase **B**. Tell the class that "Mr. Spelling B" has a very large family with 25 other members. Ask students what other members they think are in Mr. Spelling B's family. Display an assortment of lowercase letters to aid in the discussion.

Directions

1. Tell students that it is important to correct spelling as part of editing. Writing is easier for someone to read and understand when words are spelled correctly.

2. Review with students the words for which you hold them responsible (e.g., the 100 high frequency words on page 115). Distribute student copies of high frequency word bookmarks (if your students do not already have something similar) as a reference tool.

3. Distribute copies of "Washing the Car" (page 114). Have students circle any misspelled words in the paragraph. (There are five misspelled words in the paragraph.) They will then write each word correctly above the misspelled word.

Closing

Ask students how they determined which words in the sample were misspelled. Did they know and remember the word? Did they use the sentence to see if it made sense? Did they carefully look at the word to see if it looked correct? Did they use the high frequency words bookmark as a reference tool?

Extension

Play a "Mr. Spelling B" game. Divide the class into two teams. Read aloud "Mr. Spelling B's House" (page 114). As you read, stop after underlined words and ask a member of each team, in turn, to correctly say and spell the word. If the person spells the word correctly, the team receives a point.

©Teacher Created Resources, Inc.

Conventions Trait

Washing the Car

by Caleb V.

I washed the car whith my dad and brother. We used a hose, rag, and soap. We washed it clen. It was easier because it went faster than it woud by myself. Wee worked very well together. My dad used th hose. My brother and I wiped the car with soap.

Mr. Spelling B's House

Yesterday I decided to go see <u>my</u> friend, Mr. Spelling B. <u>On</u> the way to his house, I saw a cat. I know Mr. B. <u>has</u> a cat. When I got there I asked <u>him</u> if he lost his cat. He <u>said</u> no, and showed me his cat <u>up</u> on the porch. We decided to sit on the porch to talk. Mr. B. has <u>only</u> one chair so I sat on a step. I told him he needs <u>two</u> chairs. He laughed and asked me <u>where</u> he could put <u>them</u>, the porch was so small. I guess he <u>will</u> have to build a new porch first! I <u>said</u> good-bye to <u>my</u> friend and walked <u>down</u> the sidewalk to go home.

Conventions Trait

100 High Frequency Words

a	do	in	no	than	was
about	down	into	not	that	water
after	each	is	now	the	way
all	find	it	of	their	we
an	first	its	on	them	were
and	for	just	one	then	what
are	from	know	only	there	when
as	had	like	or	these	where
at	has	little	other	this	which
be	have	long	out	time	who
been	he	made	over	to	will
but	her	make	people	too	with
by	him	many	said	two	words
called	his	may	see	up	would
can	how	more	she	use	you
could	I	most	so	very	your
did	if	my	some		

Conventions Trait

Showing the Action

Objective
Given instruction in types of verbs, students will identify action and state-of-being verbs.

Materials
- white board, overhead projector, or chart paper and marker
- "Which Type of Action?" (page 117), one copy for display
- verb cards (page 117)
- cardstock
- "Actions Speak Louder Than Words" (page 118), one copy per student (optional)

Preparation
Enlarge "Which Type of Action?" (page 117) for display. Copy the verb cards (page 117) onto cardstock and cut the cards apart.

Opening
Tell students that *action verbs* show what happens in writing, rather than just telling the reader. Ask students to offer examples of action words.

Directions
1. Continue a discussion about types of verbs. Explain *state of being verbs* as this: sometimes the subject of a sentence (person, place, or thing) is not doing any action (e.g., a girl is happy). In this case *is* operates as a state of being verb—the girl is not doing anything; *is* tells how she feels or her state of mind. However, effective writing would show what the girl does because she is happy or how she acts. Interesting writing shows action.

2. Have students play a charades game. Divide the class into two teams. The first team will draw a Verb Card and one or more students from their team will act out the action on the card. The other team will try to guess the action. Tell students there may be "state of being cards," and then the student should simply be what is on the card (e.g., happy).

3. After students play the game, discuss any verbs or concepts with which the students had difficulty. Each team could choose one or more verbs to act out for the other team.

Closing
Display "Which Type of Action?" (page 117). Have students identify the verb in each sentence and state whether the verb is an action verb or a state of being verb.

Extension
Distribute copies of "Actions Speak Louder Than Words" (page 118). Direct the students to color each stick figure and write an action verb below it. Then have the students cut out the cards and use them to write a story featuring the actions of the stick figure. Students may illustrate their story by attaching each card in the appropriate place.

Which Type of Action?

My dad plays the guitar.
Everyone in my family reads books.
Our family has a pet.
We live in a small house.
Two people are twins.

Verb Cards

is sad	laughs	thinking
is grumpy	reading	skipping
sitting	watches TV	is nice

Conventions Trait

Actions Speak Louder Than Words

Conventions Trait

What Is a Paragraph?

Objective
Given instruction in paragraph structure, students will determine paragraph breaks for a written piece.

Materials
- white board, overhead projector, or chart paper and marker
- visor pattern (page 122)
- cardstock
- stapler or tape
- construction-paper strip, 2" x 10" (5 cm x 25.5 cm), one per student
- "My Interesting Family" (page 121), one copy for display
- "You Be the Editor" (page 123), one copy per student
- student work (completed stories) from previous lessons (optional)

Preparation
Photocopy the visor pattern (page 122) onto cardstock. Cut the visors out. Enlarge "My Interesting Family" (page 121) for display.

Opening
Distribute the visors and strips of construction paper. Tell students they will be editors today and will need the kind of hat an editor might wear. Have students decorate their visor if desired. Demonstrate how to attach a construction-paper strip to the visor to make a headband. Staple strips to fit students or have students tape their own.

Directions
1. Ask students if they know anything about what editors do in their job. Define *editor* as "someone who corrects and revises writing to get it ready for publication."

2. Ask students to review what specific aspects of writing they will need to edit (e.g., spelling, punctuation, capitalization).

3. Tell the class that editors also check for appropriate paragraphs and titles.

4. Teach or review basic paragraph structure. A paragraph should have a topic sentence, sentences with details, and a closing sentence. Each paragraph should have just one main idea; if a new idea is introduced, a new paragraph should be started.

Conventions Trait

What Is a Paragraph? *(cont.)*

Directions *(cont.)*

5. Display "My Interesting Family" (page 121) and read it aloud. Discuss each paragraph division.

6. Discuss the concept of appropriate titles with the students   A title should relate to the idea(s) in the writing. Effective titles catch the reader's attention without being too long or confusing. Ask students whether or not the title for the sample paragraph is appropriate and why.

7. Distribute copies of "You Be the Editor" (page 123). Have students mark each place where a new paragraph should begin. Students should also give the piece an appropriate title.

Closing

Go over the correct paragraph divisions for page 123 with the class. Check for student understanding. Ask a few students to read their titles. Have the class vote on the most appropriate title for the piece.

Extension

Distribute copies of student work (e.g., completed stories) from previous lessons. Have students edit their work for all of the conventions learned. You might want students to use a different color for spelling, punctuation, capitals, etc.

My Interesting Family

by Holly F.

I have a very big family. My dad's side has 48 people. I have two grandmas and grandpas. I also have a lot of aunts and uncles.

I go to Disneyland, the beach, and other places with my family.

I don't have a pet. But my aunt and uncle, Dakota and Sunny, have a dog.

I love my family.

Conventions Trait

Visor Pattern

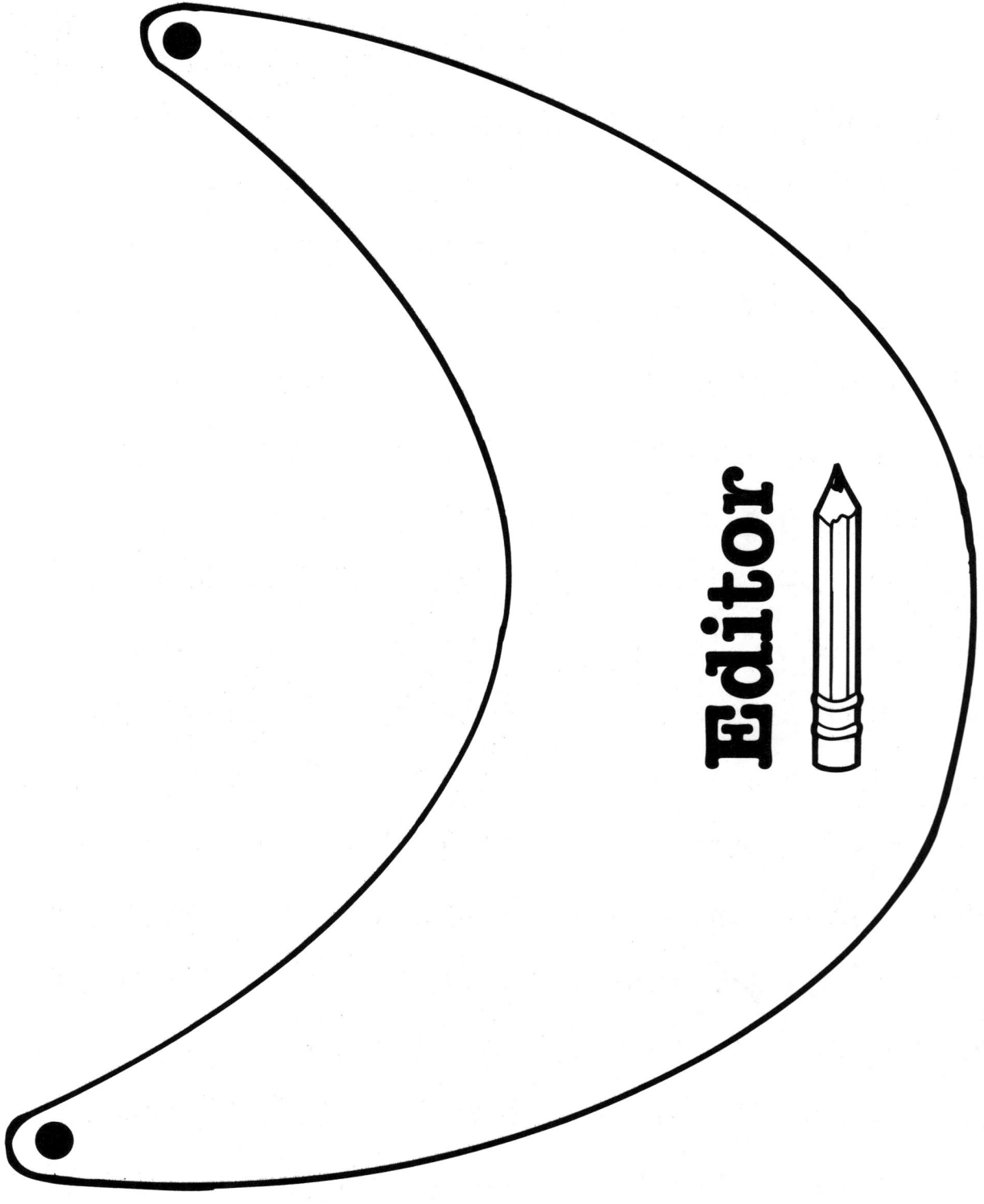

#3584 Traits of Good Writing: Grades 1–2   122   ©Teacher Created Resources, Inc.

You Be the Editor

_____

by Brian M.

Once when I was young, my father decided to take me to the forest. First we saw foxglove flowers, then we saw a real fox! It had the sharpest teeth! But it was as tame as a kitten. So we took it home. It fed on milk and roast beef. Then one morning we took the fox for a walk. We went to the forest. The fox showed us to a large pit. All 100 foxes came to the same pit and howled. Then they stopped. All the trees fell down and monster plants began to grow! Each and every plant grew as big as our house. Then a bear tried to attack us! But the foxes and some wolves saved us. We were so grateful that we built a fort and gave it to the foxes and wolves. It was a great celebration. Then it was time to go. We left the forest and went home. Every day we came back to the forest and played with the foxes and the wolves.

Presentation

The trait of Presentation refers to the publication part of the writing process. After students have completed a written piece, they present it to their audience: visually, orally, or using both formats. The Presentation trait consists of two components: visual and auditory.

Students consider appropriate visual formats for their writing, as well as the use of color. Visual aids include charts, diagrams, and graphs. The visuals may include text. Specifically, students learn how to create a graph for a presentation.

The auditory component of Presentation includes presenting work in an oral format; students learn public speaking skills through drama and critique. Lessons also give students the opportunity to practice speaking about a personal experience, ask and respond to questions, and clearly state their main point when presenting their writing to others.

Presentation

Visual Elements

- select a presentation format
- include illustrations that catch the reader's attention
- incorporate visual aids such as photos, drawings, charts, diagrams, and graphs
- express your own ideas and reflections

Auditory Elements

- tell about experience and knowledge of the topic
- ask and respond to questions
- have a clear main point when speaking to others
- read writing to others
- make eye contact while giving oral presentations
- organize your ideas for oral presentations (i.e., include content appropriate to the audience, use notes, summarize main points)

Presentation Trait

It Takes All Kinds

Objective

Given the opportunity to view a variety of visual layout formats, students will plan and complete a creative page using words and pictures.

Materials

- white board, overhead projector, or chart paper and marker
- "Presentation" poster (page 125), one copy for display
- magazines and other print media
- "Friends in my Life" (page 128), one copy for display
- sample scrapbook page, if available
- "Thinking about My Friend" (page 129), one copy per student
- construction-paper scraps, decorative scissors, rulers, markers, stickers, and other craft supplies

Preparation

Enlarge the "Presentation" poster (page 125) and "Friends in My Life" (page 128) for display.

Opening

Show students a variety of magazine pages or other print media. Ask them what catches their attention and interest in the advertisements and stories. Draw the students' attention to the "Presentation" poster (page 125). Explain that you will focus on the visual aspects of Presentation first.

Directions

1. Discuss the different ways magazine pages portray words, pictures, lines, and color. Point out to students how text and pictures are arranged on various pages.

2. Show the students "Friends in My Life" (page 128). Ask which arrangement of text and pictures seems most effective and why. Discuss instances in which each individual layout would be most effective (e.g., a sidebar when the article contains specific points the author wants the reader to remember).

3. Ask how many students have seen a scrapbook page. Show a sample scrapbook page, if available. Explain that scrapbook pages combine many forms of media, such as colored paper, different kinds of lines, letters, pictures, photographs, or drawings, to present a main idea.

4. Distribute copies of "Thinking about My Friend" (page 129). Explain that students will use this page to plan how they will format a scrapbook page about their friend(s). Go over each aspect of the planning sheet with the class, answering any questions the students may have. Discuss various ways to format a page for effectiveness, based on which aspect of the page students wish to emphasize. Model how to complete part of the page.

It Takes All Kinds *(cont.)*

Directions *(cont.)*

5. Have students use page 129 to plan their scrapbook page. Remind students that their page will include two or three sentences that describe their friend(s).

Closing

Monitor and assist students as they complete their scrapbook page. You might want to have the students check the effectiveness of their layout with you or another student before they glue anything on the page.

Extension

Have students use one of the patterns below to create an award for a special friend. Set out a variety of craft supplies for student use. Students should plan the best way to design the award before drawing, coloring, or adding text. Students may cut the award into a special shape and present it to their friend during a class sharing time.

Presentation Trait

Friends in My Life

Friends I Play With

Susie

Jimmy

Gerry

Isaac

Friends at School

I like to play with Kayla and Logan at school.

Friends in My Community

I like to go to the library each week. The librarians help me find neat books!

Miss Margaret

Mr. John

Friends I Talk To

After school, I go home and play with my neighborhood friends. We talk about everything that happened that day!

Presentation Trait

Thinking about My Friend

1. Write two or three sentences about a friend.
_____
_____
_____

2. What border will I use on my page? (straight, wavy, other lines, dots, designs, etc.)
_____

3. What pictures will I use on my page? (drawings, photographs, pictures from magazines, etc.)
_____
_____

4. What other decoration will I use on my page? (bits of colored paper in different shapes, stickers, glitter, markers, etc.)
_____
_____

5. How will I organize my page so it will look neat? Where will I put each item? Draw a sample page in the box below showing where you will put writing, pictures, and decoration.
_____

Presentation Trait

Now I See It

Objective

Given instruction in visual aids (specifically graphs), students will collect data and make an accurate graph.

Materials

- white board, overhead projector, or chart paper and markers
- sample graphs for display (i.e., from a math lesson)
- "My Favorite Book Graph" (page 131), one copy for display
- "My Friends Like to Play" (page 132), one copy per student
- cardstock, 9" x 12" (23 cm x 30 cm), one sheet per student
- index cards (optional)

Preparation

Enlarge "My Favorite Book Graph" (page 131) for display.

Opening

Refer students to the Visual portion of the "Presentation" poster (page 125). Ask students what they know about visual aids. Explain that visual aids are things a reader can see that help explain writing or help someone understand the writing better. Tell the class that they will learn about visual aids and will practice making a graph, one form of a visual aid.

Directions

1. Show the class the sample graphs. Tell students that a visual aid may be a chart, a graph, a diagram, or a picture. Each visual aid shows a specific type of information. Authors will choose a visual aid to use based on the information they want to call attention to or emphasize.

2. Display the "My Favorite Book Graph" (page 131). Ask students to tell what they notice about the graph. What information does it show? How would this graph be helpful in a class presentation?

3. Explain how to make a bar graph. Across the bottom of a page, the graph will be divided into sections, or bars, to show the various choices or options. For example, if the graph shows favorite flavors of ice cream, across the bottom of the graph there will be one division for each flavor from which respondents choose. Along the side of the page, usually the left side, the graph is divided into numerical increments to show how many respondents selected a particular option. For a first graph, students should number the divisions by one's; on subsequent graphs or for surveys involving many respondents, students may wish to number by five's or ten's. You may want to demonstrate how to make a graph on the white board as you discuss the process.

Presentation Trait

Now I See It (cont.)

Directions (cont.)

4. Ask students where and how an author gets information to make a graph (asks other people). Tell the students they will each take a survey among their friends to determine which games their friends like to play the most.

5. Distribute copies of "My Friends Like to Play" (page 132). Read through the survey portion of the page with the class. Have each student survey friends to gather responses to create a graph. If necessary, have students use this page the following day to complete the activity.

Closing

Have students set up the graph on cardstock. They should mark off sections on the bottom of the page for the game choices on their survey. Students will also number the left side of the graph to show how many of their friends chose each game option.

Have students use the data they collected to create a graph of games their friends like to play. Students should use color and work neatly to complete the graph.

Extension

Give each student one or two index cards. Ask students to write sentences to go with their graph telling what they learned from their friends about the games they like to play.

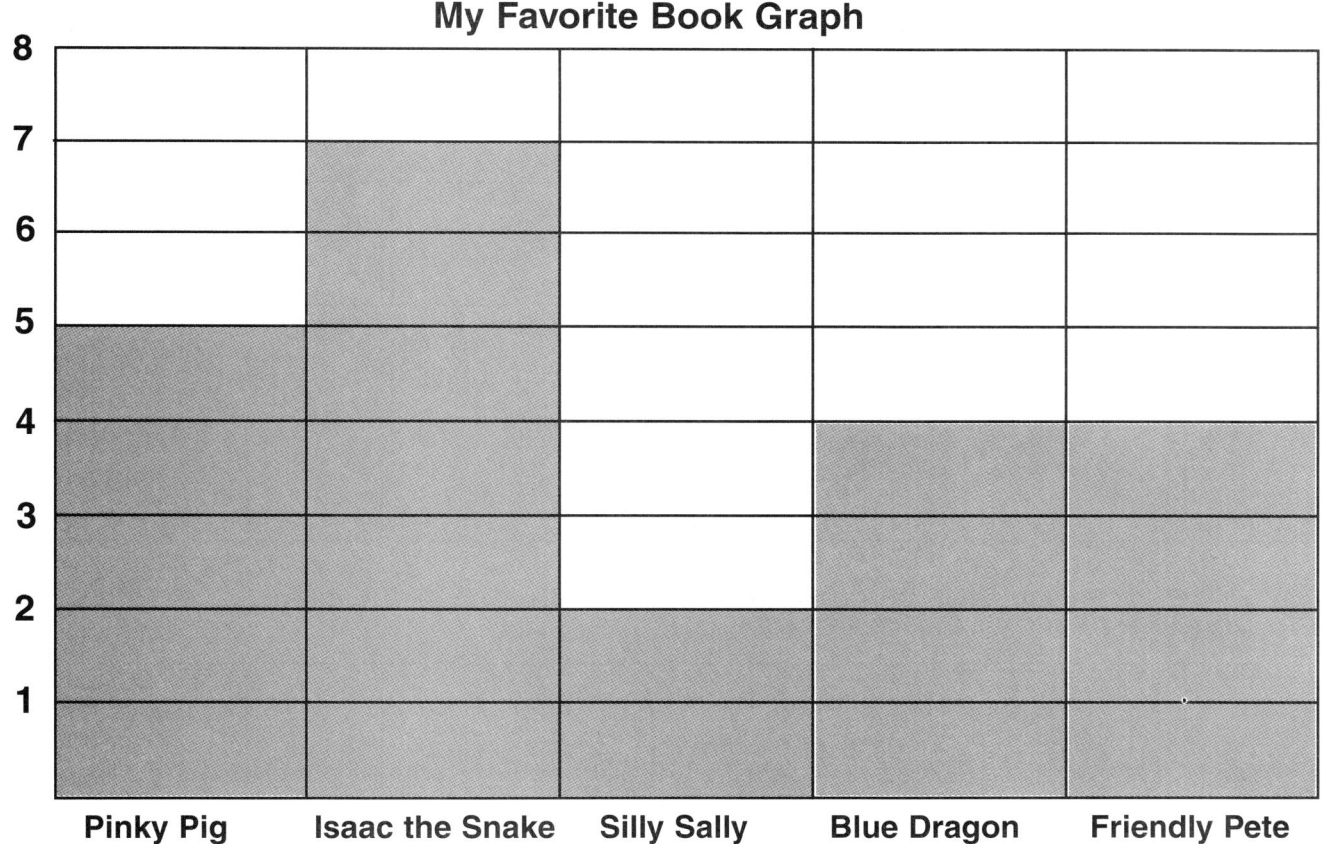

Presentation Trait

My Friends Like to Play

Survey Questions

Ask your friends these questions. Color in a box below the sport that matches each friend's favorite.

Do you like to play soccer?

Do you like to play basketball?

Do you like to play baseball?

Do you like to play hopscotch?

Do you like to play jump rope?

Do you like to play four square?

Presentation Trait

Connecting with My Friend

Objective

Given a discussion on experiences people might have with their friends, learners will write a reflective paragraph about experiences they have had with their friends and will compare their experiences with a classmate's.

Materials

- photographs or greeting cards (showing friends doing things together)
- "Playing by the Creek" (page 135)
- "Different and Alike" (page 136), one copy per student

Opening

Review with students the Visual portion of the "Presentation" poster (page 125). Tell the class there is one more characteristic that applies to both visual and auditory elements of the trait: expressing your own ideas and reflections. Explain that *ideas* refer to a person's thoughts or what they imagine in their mind, and *reflection* means to think carefully about something.

Directions

1. Show photographs or pictures of friends doing things together. Ask students to quietly think about the things they like to do with their friends, not just games they play at recess but other things as well. What special experiences have they had with their friend? Ask students to imagine this in their minds—to see a mental picture of something they have done with their friend that they really enjoyed.

2. Read aloud "Playing by the Creek" (page 135). If time permits, have students draw a picture showing the experience with a friend the author describes. Have students discuss the writing. How well does the writer express his ideas? Does the writing show that the author thought carefully about the topic before writing? How?

3. Have students recall any experiences with their friends that came to mind when you first showed the photographs. Have them write a paragraph, describing a special experience they have had with a friend. Remind the class to include details and specific words to portray a visual image to the reader.

4. Distribute copies of "Different and Alike" (page 136). Explain the use of a Venn diagram, if necessary. A student writes his or her unique experiences on one side of the diagram, labeled with his or her name. The student's partner writes his or her unique experiences on the other side of the diagram, labeled with his or her name. In the overlapping section, partners should write any experiences they have in common.

Presentation Trait

Connecting with My Friend *(cont.)*

Closing

Pair students with a partner to share their experiences and complete the Venn diagram. If time permits, pairs may share their findings with a larger group of students or with the class.

Extension

Have students write questions they could ask to interview a friend. For this activity, you might wish to pair each student with a partner he or she doesn't know well. Allow time for students to conduct the interviews and then introduce their "new friend" to the class.

Playing by the Creek

by Noah T.

Once I went camping with my family, and my friend came with us. We camped by a large creek. The creek had a lot of rocks in the water and the current was very swift. We fished for trout, but our lines got tangled in the rocks more often than we caught fish. We also found some leaves that were so big we could wear them for hats! We put the leaves on our heads, and my dad took a picture of us sitting on rocks laughing. I will always remember that camping trip.

Presentation Trait

Different and Alike

_____   _____

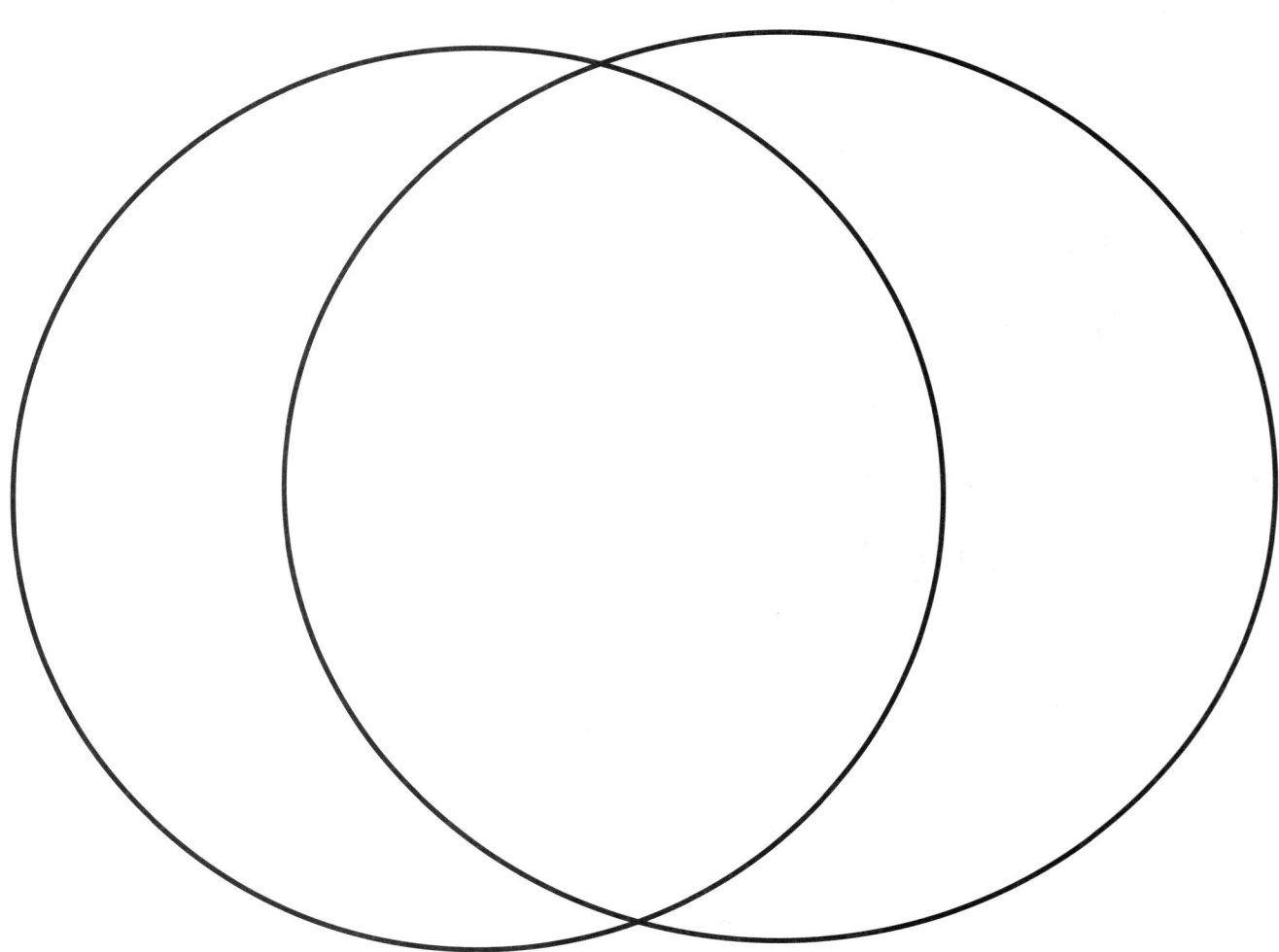

Presentation Trait

Help Us Understand You

Objective

Given instruction in public speaking skills, students will evaluate the teacher during a role-play listening activity.

Materials

- white board, overhead projector, or chart paper and marker
- "How Is My Speaking Today?" (page 139), one copy for display and one copy per student
- "Playing Soccer" (page 138)
- puppets (optional)

Preparation

Enlarge "How Is My Speaking Today?" (page 139) for display.

Opening

Draw the students' attention to the Auditory portion of the "Presentation" poster (page 125). Tell the class that Presentation includes oral, or spoken, components as well as visual or written components. Explain that an effective oral presentation is well organized and appropriate for the audience. The presentation should have a clear main point. The person presenting should make eye contact with the audience while speaking, rather than reading from a paper; however, a speaker may use notes. Overall, the audience should be able to easily understand the speaker.

Directions

1. Display a copy of "How Is My Speaking Today?" (page 139). Tell the students that you will give a short speech or presentation to the class. Inform the students that they will have a copy of the evaluation form to grade your presentation. Read each sentence on the evaluation form aloud to the class. Explain how to mark each item and clarify as necessary.

2. Read aloud "Playing Soccer" (page 138) to the class. Read correctly in some areas and make mistakes in other areas (e.g., read too fast, read too quietly).

Closing

Distribute copies of "How Is My Speaking Today?" (page 139). Have students complete the evaluation form, based on your speaking. Ask the students whether or not the speech sounded well organized and how it could have been easier to understand. Discuss other aspects of your speech to review public speaking skills with the class.

Extension

Have the students use puppets to present short speeches to one another. Students may talk about topics they have studied in class or something about which they have special knowledge or experience. Students should ask their partners or others in a small group for feedback on their oral presentations.

Presentation Trait

Playing Soccer

by Caleb V.

It is fun playing with my friends from school. We always play boys against girls. It is not about winning but having fun. I love soccer. It makes me feel good about myself and all my friends.

Presentation Trait

How Is My Speaking Today?

Color the face to show how well you could understand each part of public speaking in the speaker's presentation.

Eye Contact: Did the speaker look at the audience?
yes   a little bit   no

Rate: Did the speaker talk too fast or too slow?
just right   too fast   too slow

Volume: Did the speaker talk too loudly or too quietly?
just right   too loud   too quiet

Organization: Did the speaker have a clear main point?
yes   somewhat   not at all

Did the speaker use notes?
yes   a little bit   no

Did the speaker read from a paper or know what to say?
knew what to say   knew a bit   read from paper

Content: Was the topic appropriate for the audience?
yes   a little bit   not at all

Audience: Did you pay attention and listen respectfully?
yes   most of the time   no

©Teacher Created Resources, Inc.   #3584 Traits of Good Writing: Grades 1–2

Presentation Trait

Presenting . . . My Friend

Objective

Given a planning guideline, students will design and create a booklet about a friend to present to the class.

Materials

- personal writing about a friend
- "My Special Friend" (page 141)
- "I'd Like to Introduce You" (page 142), one copy per student, plus extras
- markers, stickers, or other decorative items
- butcher paper or other wrapping paper, paint, sponges or brushes (optional)

Preparation

Write a short paragraph about a friend to share with the class. Include aspects of the Presentation trait: specifically personal experiences, knowledge of your friend, and a main point. Copy "My Special Friend" (page 141) onto white construction paper. Cut along the border of dotted lines. Fold the paper lengthwise and then fold along the solid lines. Unfold the paper. (You should have eight sections.) Fold the paper in half width-wise and cut along the center crease where there is a dotted line. Open the paper and fold it lengthwise again. Push the end sections together to fold into a little book. Four pages will be formed with two sides each.

Opening

Share your personal written piece about a friend. Ask students to identify which characteristics of the Presentation trait you included. Invite students to ask appropriate questions about your presentation; model and respond to students' questions.

Directions

1. Show students the "My Special Friend" booklet and read it aloud to the class. Ask how the author showed personal experience and knowledge in the writing. Have a student identify the main point.

2. Tell students they will make a booklet about their friends. After they have finished, they will present it to the class, practicing the aspects of Presentation they have learned.

3. Distribute copies of "I'd Like to Introduce You" (page 142). Show students how to cut, fold, and assemble the booklet (see Preparation section).

4. After students assemble their booklets, have them write at least one sentence about their friend on each page. They should decorate the cover and write a title for the booklet.

Closing

Have students present their booklets to the class.

Extension

Have the class make wrapping paper using butcher paper and paint. They may wrap their friend booklets and give them to a special friend.

Presentation Trait

My Special Friend

(Booklet pages, arranged for folding:)

1. My Special Friend

2. We like to eat ice cream together.

3. We like to go to the lake.

4. Sometimes we watch a DVD together.

5. My friend and I like a lot of the same things.

6. My friend listens to me and I listen to her.

7. Most of all, we just like to spend time together.

Presentation Trait

I'd Like to Introduce You

The End

by _____

1.

2.

3.

4.

5.

6.

Technology Resources

edHelper.com

http://www.edhelper.com

General reference site for lesson plans and resources for teachers. Includes printable reproducible activity pages in all subject areas.

Education Resource Information Center

http://www.eric.ed.gov

Database of educational journal articles. Search using "writing traits" or "6+1 Trait writing." Or search by document #ED481235 or #ED485670 for specific articles with an overview of 6+1 Trait™ writing.

The Educator's Reference Desk

http://www.eduref.org

General teaching reference site. Includes articles, resources, links, and lesson plans for all subject areas.

Kent (Washington) School District

http://www.kent.k12.wa.us

Click on "Curriculum" on the left sidebar. Then click on "more," then "writing." A wealth of resources on 6+1 Trait™ writing, including an overview chart of the traits, lesson plans, and assessment. Includes resources for other content areas sorted by grade level.

The Northwest Regional Educational Laboratory

http://www.nwrel.org

The "parent" of 6+1 Trait™ writing; researchers first identified and defined effective writing traits at this regional educational laboratory. Offers definitions of the traits, trait prompts, tips for teachers, lesson plans, and assessment scoring guides.

TeachersFirst.com

http://www.teachersfirst.com

Overall resource site for teachers. Offers content matrix to search lesson plans in various subject areas.

Teachers Net

http://www.teachers.net

General reference site, specifically for lesson plans. Click on lesson plans on the home page, then on subject area. Lessons sorted by general subject area or grade levels only.

Web English Teacher

http://www.webenglishteacher.com

Click on "Writing" on the left sidebar to find articles, lesson plans, and assessment resources for using 6+1 Trait™ writing in the classroom.

Writing Fix

http://www.writingfix.com

Click on "6+1 Traits" on the left sidebar for a variety of helpful resources.

General Search Engines

To search a general search engine, such as *http://www.google.com*, use key phrase "6+1 Trait writing" to retrieve several links.

Answer Key

Page 90

(transition words are in bold type)

One year there was a famine. I was unusually unhappy. I was starved. **So** I went on a walk to see if there were any berries. **But** I found no berries. I found a seed pack. **Then** I put one seed into the ground. **When** I woke up in the morning, I saw a tree. It had an orange on it. I said I wish it had apples, and the tree burst out with apples. **Then** I said grapes, watermelon, pineapple, and cantaloupe. All of them came bursting out on the tree. **Finally** we sold all the fruit and got so much money we built a store.

Page 98

Plants start from seeds.
They need water and sunlight to grow.
Then flowers bud and bloom.
After they bloom, flowers die and fall off.
Seeds from the flower drop in the ground, and a new flower grows.

Page 108

My family includes **Doug, Tracie, Brian,** and me. **Dad** works on computers. **Mom** goes to **Cascade College.** My family likes to play games and cook. **Grandma** and **Grandpa** and I like to cook, read, and go shopping at **Bird** in **Hand.** I have a pet named **Nala.** She likes kids, bones, and her master. I go to **Hearthwood School.**

Kenneth M.

Page 112

1. ?
2. !
3. .
4. !
5. .
6. ?

Page 114

(corrected words are in bold type)

I washed the car **with** my dad and brother. We used a hose, rag, and soap. We washed it **clean**. It was easier because it went faster than it **would** by myself. **We** worked very well together. My dad used **the** hose. My brother and I wiped the car with soap.

Page 123

Once when I was young, my father decided to take me to the forest. First we saw foxglove flowers, then we saw a real fox! It had the sharpest teeth! But it was as tame as a kitten.

So we took it home. It fed on milk and roast beef. Then one morning we took the fox for a walk. We went to the forest. The fox showed us to a large pit. All 100 foxes came to the same pit and howled. Then they stopped.

All the trees fell down and monster plants began to grow! Each and every plant grew as big as our house.

Then a bear tried to attack us! But the foxes and some wolves saved us. We were so grateful that we built a fort and gave it to the foxes and wolves. It was a great celebration. Then it was time to go.

We left the forest and went home. Every day we came back to the forest and played with the foxes and the wolves.